The New Face of America

The New Face of America

How the Emerging Multiracial, Multiethnic Majority Is Changing the United States

Eric J. Bailey

 PRAEGER

AN IMPRINT OF ABC-CLIO, LLC
Santa Barbara, California • Denver, Colorado • Oxford, England

Library of Congress Cataloging-in-Publication Data

Bailey, Eric J., 1958–
    The new face of America : how the emerging multiracial, multiethnic majority is changing the United States / Eric J. Bailey.
        pages cm
    Includes bibliographical references and index.
    ISBN 978–0–313–38569–8 (cloth : acid-free paper) — ISBN 978–0–313–38570–4 (ebook)
1. Racially mixed people—United States. 2. Cultural pluralism—United States. 3. Social change—United States. 4. United States—Race relations. 5. United States—Ethnic relations. 6. United States—Population. 7. United States—Social conditions—1980– I. Title.
E184.A1B233   2013
305.8′050073—dc23   2012048978

ISBN: 978–0–313–38569–8
EISBN: 978–0–313–38570–4

17 16 15 14 13   1 2 3 4 5

This book is also available on the World Wide Web as an eBook.
Visit www.abc-clio.com for details.

Praeger
An Imprint of ABC-CLIO, LLC

ABC-CLIO, LLC
130 Cremona Drive, P.O. Box 1911
Santa Barbara, California 93116-1911

This book is printed on acid-free paper ∞

Manufactured in the United States of America

Although I have admired and respected all of my older brothers, this book is dedicated to two of my four older brothers—Ronnie Bailey and Dwight Eugene Bailey. In my early years growing up in Springfield, Ohio, I tended to be protected and looked after by my brother Ronnie, eight years my elder. He was always around to lend a helping hand. Although we parted ways during my elementary, middle school, high school, and college years, we've maintained our closeness. We are even closer since the passing of his always-caring wife, Debbie.

My brother Dwight is four years older than me and has always been my best friend. Growing up in Springfield and Wilberforce, Ohio, I could always count on him to help me with things important at each stage of my early childhood and young adulthood. He gave me confidence, reassurance, and motivation to be the best that I could be at anything that I wanted to try.

I admire Dwight for being the charismatic, fun-loving, and talkative person whom he has always been.

I especially admire Dwight for taking a stance during the mid-1970s to enter into an interracial relationship when a lot of people did not think it was the right thing to do. I knew that he had made the right decision to marry his wife, Angela. I still (literally) look up to and admire him.

Contents

PART IV. FUTURE TRENDS

Preface

The New Face of America: How the Emerging Multiracial, Multiethnic Majority Is Changing the United States examines some of the most significant issues associated with "multiracials" today. Despite their increased—and still increasing—numbers across recent decades, there seems to be a total lack of recognition of this group, and of its importance in our society.

In my journey to better understand their issues, I first reflected upon my own personal history. I was exposed to some of these issues throughout my adolescent and early adult years. As an African American raised in the Midwestern state of Ohio during the 1960s and 1970s, my mother always expressed her multiracial, multiethnic heritage. My brothers and I were taught that all of us had relatives of mixed heritage (Native American, French, Creole, and European) and that this mix contributed to the wide diversity of our physical features.

Although this multiracial heritage was brought to my attention in my childhood years, it was not until one of my older brothers decided to have an interracial relationship and marriage that some of these real-life multiracial issues hit home. I admired how my older brother, his wife, and their kids adapted to a world that was, and still is, struggling to embrace them both individually and collectively as a family.

In the past, if individuals or families were biracial/multiracial and had some type of African American heritage (the so-called one-drop rule), their issues were assumed to be primarily African American ones. Today, many biracial and multiracial individuals and families do not adhere to this one-drop rule. I have always felt that the one-drop rule was wrong, discriminatory, and racist. It especially goes against the common right of equality associated with all groups. This is one of many issues addressed in this book.

Chapter 1 presents the premise of the book and highlights the significance of the growing multiracial populations in the United States. This opening chapter proposes that the major causes of these groups' growth involve an increase in interracial relations and the new cultural trend of openly acknowledging one's multiracial heritage. The chapter concludes with a personal account from one of my key "multiracial informants," as I will call them.

Chapter 2 examines and compares the 2000 and 2010 U.S. census data. These census data firmly established the existence and growth of multiracial populations in the United States.

Chapter 3 investigates how multiracials sometimes struggle with their identity and the major factors influencing their self-identity. Different types of multiracial families are highlighted.

Chapter 4 examines the cultural history of multiracialism in America. This chapter highlights specifically the issues connected with those persons who were socially identified as mulattos, mixed bloods, mestizos, Amerasians, and hapas.

Chapter 5 reviews the one-drop rule and its historical effect on African Americans. This chapter also examines this concept's cultural impact on multiracials and explains how many multiracials have rejected it.

Chapter 6 discusses the topic of race and examines the preferred physical features among racial and ethnic populations in the United States. This chapter contends that multiracial physical features have dramatically influenced the preference for certain types of physical features among other racial and ethnic populations.

Chapter 7 highlights some of the major health disparity issues associated with multiracials and discusses the interrelationship of race, ancestry, and genetics with health outcomes. Multiracials' views on race-based therapies are also presented.

Chapter 8 addresses the challenges that many multiracials experience when they require bone marrow transplants. Because there are so few bone marrow donors who can match the specific blood type of certain multiracials, an exact bone marrow match is difficult to find.

Chapter 9 addresses the issue of transracial adoption both from the parents' perspective and from the child/adult's perspective. A new model with a cultural approach for understanding and solving transracial adoption issues is presented.

Chapter 10 recognizes the accomplishments of a number of multiracial celebrities who have had a direct impact in the movie industry, sports, television news journalism, and politics. This chapter also highlights the charitable causes and organizations that have benefited, and further spread the fruits of success, from these celebrities.

Chapter 11 examines how multiracials have been treated around the globe, paying special attention to their roles in Europe, Africa, Asia, and South and Central America.

Chapter 12 presents insightful comments, opinions, values, and beliefs from key multiracial informants who were interviewed for this book. Here multiracials speak out on a wide variety of issues.

Finally, Chapter 13 speculates on the future of our world, when multiracials and multiethnics become the majority. A scenario of the world in the year 2100 is presented.

Acknowledgments

This book would not have been possible without the insight and expertise from my key experts. I sincerely thank my very good friends Mayella Valero (who assisted with the design of the questionnaire), Millie Nunez, Corey Patin, Johnathan Hilbert, and Anthony Kulukulualani. I also thank organizations including Multiracial Americans, Blended People America, and Multiracial Heritage Week.

In addition, I thank the two outstanding libraries at East Carolina University—the J. Y. Joyner Library and the William E. Laupus Health Sciences Library—for their excellent research journals, online services, and book collections, as well as their outstanding directors and administrative staff. I also thank both libraries for recognizing my two previous books with two book awards.

I also thank all of the students who have taken my classes over the years. Each year, I reach another level of enjoyment, learning, and challenge from the students in my classes. They give me inspiration and hope that our future leaders will have the capability to make our world a better place.

Of course, my journey in academia and the federal government would not have been possible without support, commitment, and sacrifice from my immediate family—my very intelligent, entrepreneurial, artistic, beautiful wife Gloria Jean Harden; my double-major (Art and English) daughter Ebony; my soccer-talented, college-bound son Darrien; and my golf-talented, science-focused middle-school son Marcus. I am very blessed to have my family.

I also feel blessed to have been raised by two incredible, pioneering, motivating, disciplined, and loving parents—Jean Ethel Ballew and Roger William Bailey, Jr. They have been, and always will be, my heart and soul.

In addition, I feel blessed to have brothers Dwight, Ronnie, Billie, and Michael Bailey. All have a special place in my heart and have played a significant role in my upbringing. I am most grateful. And I am honored to have been a part of the lives of Dwight's family members—his wife Angela, son Darrick, and daughter Alicia.

I also want to thank six musical artists and their songs that inspired me throughout the writing of this book—Vanessa Williams (*Comfort Zone* and *Next*), Sade (*Soldier of Love* and *The Ultimate Collection*), the late Tina Marie (*It Must Be Magic*), Luther Vandross (*Give Me the Reason*), Whitney Houston (*Whitney*), and Michael Jackson (*Invincible* and *History*).

This is my sixth book with Greenwood Publishing/Praeger. It has been another fascinating and enlightening journey, both in writing this book and in working with the publisher's new parent company—ABC-CLIO. I sincerely thank again my outstanding, patient, and remarkable editor Debbie Carvalko for working with me on yet another book project.

In their own way, each of the people and groups listed here has provided support so I could complete this book while undertaking additional activities related to my joint-appointed full professor position at East Carolina University. As the writing of this book began, I became director of an innovative academic program, "The Ethnic and Rural Health Disparities (ERHD) Graduate Certificate Online Program." That position meant a new commitment to the academia I have served across more than 30 years of scholarly and professional activity, including years at Miami University (Ohio), Wayne State University (Detroit, Michigan), University of Houston, Indiana University (IUPUI, Indianapolis), Emory University, University of Arkansas Medical Sciences, Charles Drew University of Medicine and Science, the Centers for Disease Control and Prevention, and the National Institutes of Health.

I deeply appreciate that my decades-long journey might not have been so fruitful, rewarding, and energizing if not for the friends, family, scholars, and yes, sometimes musicians—all together a strongly multiracial group of supporters—who have been my own "team" in learning, in teaching, in writing, and in life.

PART I

Overview and Current Issues

ONE

How the Emerging Multiracial, Multiethnic Majority Is Changing the United States

INTRODUCTION

It's the elephant in the room, yet few are paying attention to this national issue sure to impact everyone's life in America. This elephant gets bigger and bigger every year, with its growth becoming particularly obvious when the United States conducts its 10-year census. Once the census is complete, government experts share the numbers with the country and still, amazingly, many Americans are quite surprised by the changing racial demographics of the United States. But be observant and there will be no surprise. Just look around your neighborhood, whether it is an urban area, suburban community, or rural area, and no matter in which state it is located. America's racial make-up is changing right before our eyes, even though few agencies, institutions, communities, professionals, and politicians acknowledge it.

For example, in 2011, after the 2010 census data collection was completed, numerous census reports were published showing dramatic increases in multiracial and multiethnic populations in the United States, particularly from 2000 to 2010. According to the 2010 U.S. Census, the kindergarten class of 2010–2011 was sociodemographically different from the 2000 kindergarten class. For example, the U.S. Department of Commerce's U.S. Bureau of Census 2010 (2011) reported that "about 25% of 5-year olds are Hispanic versus 19% in 2000." Moreover, the U.S. Bureau of Census reported that "the percentage of 5-year olds who were classified as multiracial are 3% versus 2% in 2000" (U.S. Department of Commerce U.S. Bureau of Census 2010, 2011). In general, the statistics indicate that the kindergarten class of 2010–2011 was more Hispanic/Latino, less white, and more multiracial than in 2000 (U.S. Department of Commerce, United States Census 2010, 2011). These percentage changes directly show that the United States is changing racially and ethnically.

In an article entitled "Census: Whites Make up Minority of Babies in U.S." published in *USA Today* (2011), the author stated the following: "Demographers say the numbers provide the clearest confirmation yet of a changing social order, one in which racial and ethnic minorities will become the U.S. majority by midcentury."

Finally, in another U.S. Department of Commerce, U.S. Bureau of Census 2010 (2011) report, demographers examined changing household composition, place of residence, marital patterns, and multiracial awareness issues. The major themes of this report were as follows: (1) families are more diverse in their living arrangements; (2) the average household will increase because of the influx of immigrants; (3) households with children younger than age 18 will decline; (4) men and women are significantly delaying marriage (women typically marry at age 26 years and men at age 28 years) because they are more frequently obtaining higher educational degrees; (5) more Americans are suburbanites; (6) more Americans live in the South (37%) and West (23%) than in the Midwest; (7) the Hispanic/Latino population has doubled in size; (8) more individuals are identifying themselves as multiracial—now 2 percent of the total population, up from 1.6 percent in 2000; and (9) interracial marriage is increasing, such that 1 in 7 new marriages now includes spouses of different racial or ethnic backgrounds (U.S. Department of Commerce, U.S. Bureau of Census 2010, 2011).

In reviewing these three U.S. Bureau of Census 2010 reports, three major questions arise that most Americans are asking regarding recent changing demographics in the United States over the past two decades:

1. Why are there more multiracials?
2. What is really causing the increase in the multiracial and multiethnic populations?
3. What will the United States look like racially in the near future?

CAUSES FOR INCREASES IN MULTIRACIAL POPULATIONS

The United States grew, developed, and organized itself into one of the most powerful westernized countries in the world primarily owing to the intellect, hard work ethic, and togetherness, spirituality, and belief systems of the many different types of peoples who moved to the country over the centuries. Today's Americans are the result of centuries of immigrant nationalities, indentured servants, slaves, and people fleeing persecution from their homelands coming loosely together to form the great nation that we call "the United States."

Yet one segment of the U.S. population has continued to be overlooked and not really largely recognized for its contributions to the growth and development of our nation—namely, those individuals identified as "multiracial." So what does it mean for an individual to identify himself or herself as "multiracial," or belonging to more than one race, in the United States today?

Multiracial is defined as follows:

- Made up of, involving, or acting on behalf of various races
- Having ancestors of several or various races
- People whose ancestries come from multiple races (Root 1996)

Other terms used similarly to "multiracial" are "biracial" and "transracial." Definitions of these terms, along with others used in this book, are highlighted in the Glossary.

A key premise of this book is that the major cause of the dramatic increase in the number of multiracials in the United States involves primarily two factors:

- A significant increase in interracial relations and marriages
- A new cultural trend of recognizing and accepting one's multiracial and multiethnic heritage

New Cultural Trend

Although individuals have been increasingly identifying themselves as multiracial for a number of years, it was not until the U.S. Census 2000 that individuals could self-identify with two or more races. For example, according to Schmitt (2001), statistics from the U.S. Census 2000 showed "two million or 5% more said they belong to more than one race as opposed to the 1990 census and this increase [was] higher than initially projected." Schmitt (2001) also reported that the increase in multiracials involved an increasing number of blacks "in interracial marriages and younger blacks identifying themselves as multiracial."

Among all Americans since 2000, the number of individuals who identify themselves as belonging to more than one race has increased by 33 percent. According to Schmitt (2001), "their growth is a reflection of the changing populational patterns within our society and a greater acceptance of the term 'multiracial'." In the 2000 census, those individuals who preferred to check more than one race on the census form and to embrace multiracialism tended to be younger than age 18 (Schmitt 2001).

This new cultural trend of acknowledging and recognizing one's multiracial heritage was also influenced, of course, by the United States' election of its first multiracial president—Barack Obama. Initially, the country became aware of Obama's multiracial heritage when he was a Democratic presidential candidate. In fact, Obama published two best-selling books that highlighted his multiracial background, which not only helped American voters to better understand his background and political perspective, but also enabled the American people to feel comfortable with a potential president of a multiracial background.

However, when then-presidential candidate Barack Obama was questioned by multiracial supporters about his racial identity in 2008, he stated that he self-identified himself as an African American. This should be the end of the story, right?

When the 2010 census was conducted, this issue reemerged and many groups (multiracials and African Americans) wondered which racial category President Obama self-selected as his racial identity. As the days unfolded following his self-selection in April, the White House was initially low key in sharing this information with the general public. Eventually, then-Press Secretary Robert Gibbs announced that President Obama self-selected his race as "African American."

Consider how significant it would have been if President Obama had selected "multiracial" as his race on the 2010 census form. Perhaps all those who had identified themselves as multiracial would have instantly felt more "culturally accepted" by mainstream society, simply because the president of the United States self-identified himself as multiracial. We know that once a president recognizes, supports, or signs off on an issue, it becomes culturally engrained in the total fabric of U.S. society—symbolically, socially, economically, educationally, historically, politically, religiously, and racially. Thus, from that moment on, multiracial status might well have been changed forever in the United States.

However, that did not happen in 2010. The president, along with millions of other individuals who could have selected the box "multiracial," preferred to select another racial classification. Some say the president adhered to the same old African American racial categorization pattern referred to as the "one-drop rule."

Couple the increasingly popular cultural trend of embracing a multiracial label with the fact that much of the fast growth in diversity has been driven by an influx of young immigrants, whose birth rates are higher than those of non-Hispanic whites, and increased interracial marriages, and we have to recognize that the multiracial population is actually driving the U.S. population growth. Nationally, the multiracial population comprises approximately 6.8 million Americans, or 2.4 percent of the total population. The state with the largest multiracial population is Hawaii (24.1%), followed by Alaska (5.4%). In contrast, the states with the smallest numbers of multiracials (less than 1% of the total population) are Mississippi, West Virginia, Maine, Alabama, and South Carolina.

What are the races most identified when people select "multiracial" as their category in the census? The U.S. Department of Commerce, U.S. Bureau of Census 2010 (2011) reported that "a vast majority of Americans select two races (93.2%), a much smaller percentage (6%) select three races, and the remaining selections are even smaller (four races—0.56%, five races—0.13%, and six races—0.01%)."

The next obvious question is, What are the most frequent multiple-race combinations that Americans are identifying? Table 1.1 shows the ranking of the top 20 multiple-race selections. In reviewing Table 1.1, it becomes obvious that multiple combinations of multiracial populations have been recognized by the U.S. Census Bureau. The 2000 U.S. Census offered 63 possible racial combinations, with the number of combinations growing to 126 if the respondent also checked "Hispanic," which was defined as a culture, rather than a race.

Increase in Interracial Relationships and Marriages

What is also happening here is that the rates of intermarriage have increased dramatically and the strict social boundaries against intermarriage between racial groups are eroding. Intermarriage between members of two given ethnic groups tends to increase when the degree of social distance (i.e., occupational, educational, and residential) between them declines. Rising rates of intermarriage between groups indicate the acceptance of one another as social equals (DaCosta 2007). Once established, intermarriage tends to further erode salient boundaries between groups. When that happens, ethnicity becomes largely a symbolic identification, chosen rather than ascribed, and relatively inconsequential in one's daily life.

Table 1.1   Multiple Race Combinations by Frequency

Rank	Multiple Race Selection	Number	Percentage of Total Population	Percentage of Multiple Race Population
1	White and some other race	2,206,251	0.78%	32.32%
2	White and American Indian	1,082,683	0.38%	15.86%
3	White and Asian	868,395	0.31%	12.72%
4	White and black	784,764	0.28%	11.50%
5	Black and some other race	417,249	0.15%	6.11%
6	Asian and some other race	249,108	0.09%	3.65%
7	Black and American Indian	182,494	0.06%	2.67%
8	Asian and Hawaiian or other Pacific Islander	138,802	0.05%	2.03%
9	White and Hawaiian or other Pacific Islander	112,964	0.04%	1.65%
10	White and black and American Indian	112,207	0.04%	1.64%
11	Black and Asian	106,782	0.04%	1.56%
12	American Indian and some other race	93,842	0.03%	1.37%
13	White and Asian and Hawaiian or other Pacific Islander	89,611	0.03%	1.31%
14	American Indian and Asian	52,429	0.02%	0.77%
15	White and black and some other race	43,172	0.02%	0.63%
16	Hawaiian or other Pacific Islander and some other race	35,108	0.01%	0.51%
17	White and Asian and some other race	34,962	0.01%	0.51%
18	Black and Hawaiian or other Pacific Islander	29,876	0.01%	0.44%
19	White and American Indian and some other race	29,095	0.01%	0.43%
20	White and American Indian and Asian	23,766	0.01%	0.35%

Source: Census Scope 2009.

For example, Asians and Latinos in the United States have fairly high rates of out-marriage (compared to African Americans). Almost 30 percent of Asians (27.2%) and Latinos (28.4%) out-marry, while only 10.2 percent of blacks do. Therefore, rising rates of multiracial groupings also indicate the blending and fading of some traditional racial group boundaries.

Global Increase of Multiracials

The next questions regarding the growth of the multiracial populations are as follows:

1. Is this increased pattern of multiracials strictly a U.S. phenomenon?
2. Is similar increased prevalence of multiracials being observed in other countries?
3. How are multiracial individuals and families in other countries adapting to their society's norms regarding racial classification and social stratification?

To answer these questions, a brief review of multiracial groups in other countries is presented. Countries such as Brazil, Singapore, Malaysia, and Canada illustrate varying societal adaptations of their multiracial populations. For example, as noted by Daniel (2003), "in Brazil, multiracial groups are usually between African and Amerindian (cafuzo), East Asian (mostly Japanese), and European, African and European (mulato), and Amerindian and European (caboulo or mameluco)." The most common multiracial relationships are between Africans and Europeans and between Amerindians and Europeans; thus the majority of Brazil multiracials' origins are Amerindian, European, and African (Daniel 2003).

Because multiracial relationships have been part of Brazilian society for generations, a majority of mixed-race Brazilians do not really know their ethnic ancestry (Daniel 2003). Although Brazilian society has historically demonstrated a high level of integration, the socio-stratification between European descendants and African, Amerindian, and multiracial descendants keeps these groups visually and culturally accepted.

Singapore and Malaysia also have a fairly large portion of multiracials. Singapore has an approximate population of 4.68 million, of whom 2.4 percent are multiracial. According to Winter and Debose (2003), "the majority of inter-ethnic marriages are between Chinese and Indians and the typical marital arrangement involves an Indian groom and Chinese bride." Moreover, "the offspring of such marriages are informally known as 'Chindian' and majority of Chindians in Malaysia are usually classified as 'Indian' by the Malaysian government" (Winter and Debose 2003).

Finally, in Canada, the most recent census shows that the multiracial population accounts for approximately 1.5 percent of the total population, which represents an increase of 25 percent in multiracials since the country's previous census. According to Daniel (2003), "multiracials consist of such groups as black and South Asian, white-black, white-Latin American, white-Chinese, white-Arab, and Aboriginal and European." Collectively, these groups constitute a total mixed population that is 2.7 percent larger than the U.S. multiracial population (Daniel 2003).

From these brief global examples of multiracial populations, we can answer our previously mentioned questions. First, the increased number of multiracials is not simply a U.S. trend; it is a global trend. Second, the prevalence of multiracials is increasing in many countries other than the United States. Finally, multiracial individuals and families in other countries are continuing to successfully adapt to their countries' social and racial classifications and are developing new strategies to overcome their strict societal rules.

A MULTIRACIAL PERSONAL EXAMPLE

To better understand the multiracial issues on a more individual, personal, cultural, and historical perspective, I developed a multiracial questionnaire (MRQ) in collaboration with a friend who identified herself as a multiracial. Incorporating her suggestions, I modified the questionnaire in a number of areas and then distributed it to a number of key multiracial informants.

One of my key informants (#1) identifies herself as a multiracial Asian/Pacific Islander "Filipina" person who was born in the Philippines (a Spanish colony for more than 400 years) and whose culture has much more in common with Hispanics (in terms of food, language, roots, and religion) than with other Asians. She shared with me a wide variety of significant multiracial cultural issues that often get overlooked. For example, when asked whether a vast majority of Americans are aware of the major increase of multiracial populations that is predicted to occur in the next 20 years, she responded:

For those Americans who live in urban areas who are exposed to cultural diversity, yes, they are aware of an increasing multiracial population in the next few decades. Unfortunately, for most Americans, particularly those who live in rural settings and/or homogenous communities, they seem to be oblivious or in denial. I believe that [the] vast majority of Americans do not want to accept such a growth, which is evitable.

Interestingly, when asked if she thought more people in the United States will identify themselves as multiracial each year, she stated:

> Yes, I do believe more Americans identify themselves as multiracial. I have met many people here in California who are born to parents with different ethnic backgrounds. I find it fascinating and I believe it is part of the evolutionary process. At some point, it will be difficult for the U.S. Census to capture one's true racial/ethnic identity because as more people engage in interracial relationships, the outcome will be offspring being a mix of several races and ethnicities.

Her responses highlight the very point that I made at the outset of this chapter: the United States is changing right before our eyes, physically and culturally, and it seems as if many people and institutions are not recognizing this change.

My informant's response to a question asking why she thinks it has taken the United States so long to recognize multiracial groups was this:

> With the advent of the civil rights movement and immigration growth contributing to [an] increase and variety of ethnic groups, interracial relationships/marriages became more prominent. And the offspring resulting from such partnerships created a beautiful "conundrum." What was a system of categorizing ethnicity in "black-and-white" terms became a bit more profound and at times confusing. In general, it was "easier" to identify ethnicity in a cut-and-dried manner because a multiethnic category presented some challenges. For example, you often heard from an individual who has a white mother and black father (or vice versa) that he won't describe himself as either black or white because he is both black and white. (A beautiful conundrum indeed!)

CONCLUSION

This book spotlights questions and major issues that many Americans are wondering about, yet are not fully, openly discussing as they relate to multiracial and multiethnic populations in the United States and the world. The questions and answers presented here are highly sensitive and political for many folks because they indicate that our world, our country, our state, our city, our town, and our neighborhood are statistically and visibly changing.

This book contends that the increase in multiracial populations in the United States and the world primarily involves two major factors:

- Increases in interracial relationships and marriages
- New cultural trend in recognizing and accepting one's multiracial and multiethnic heritage

The offspring of those persons who have interracial relationships/marriages, as well as people who are migrating to the United States from other countries, are deciding to identify themselves as "multiracial" as part of a new cultural, societal, and individual trend. The current quantitative and qualitative data associated with multiracials indicate that their significant increase as a subpopulation in the United States is a cultural trend that is here to stay, whether Americans are ready for it or not.

TWO

The Multiracial Population: U.S Census Assessment

INTRODUCTION

Before any further discussion of the multiracial population, it is critical to recognize how multiracials are assessed by the U.S. federal government. Whether we like it or not, the U.S. Census categorizes all citizens in the United States in all types of sociodemographic categories, particularly by race and ethnicity. From the federal government's perspective, it is vital to know which segments of the U.S. population are underserved, underrepresented, or overrepresented in such areas as health disparity, income levels, educational attainment, and employment. These critical sociodemographic data sets on specific groups of populations help to guide local and national government policies and programs, not only for all Americans but particularly for specific segments of the U.S. population. These are also the very reasons why we need so much specific sociodemographic, health, and cultural data on one of America's new emerging populations—multiracials.

Politically, multiracials and multiracial organizations have championed their own issues on a wide variety of topics over several decades, and have finally received attention from state and federal officials. Once federal officials have more accurate assessments of the multiracial population on a state-by-state basis, they can project a type of sociodemographic profile of this burgeoning segment of the U.S. population.

Perhaps one of the most intriguing aspects of the multiracial populations' sociodemographic profile is that they are a relatively new population, as a category, which many federal officials, researchers, scholars, educators, and politicians know very little about. On the one hand, this lack of information may be a good thing because it will spur some agencies, organizations, systems, and individuals to learn more about this new population, and to develop new programs specifically for its members. On the other hand, multiracials are a segment of the population that frightens some leaders and institutions, because this group is relatively unpredictable. Multiracials are people of mixed heritage, representing all racial and ethnic populations in the United States, so they also have varied perspectives. They cannot be easily categorized and evaluated, and little to no research has been done to determine norms and common thinking patterns or actions among the members of this diverse group. Some believe this may be one of the primary reasons why the U.S. federal government took so long to recognize them. Politically, multiracials are unpredictable because they have so many different backgrounds, so their opinions are not easily pegged. These multiple voices, opinions, and lifestyles make many demographers and politicians feel unable to predict their future actions.

But the time has arrived for Americans as a whole to recognize how multiracials are greatly changing life, both in the United States and worldwide.

THE 2000 U.S. CENSUS: THE FIRST OFFICIAL RECOGNITION OF MULTIRACIALS

Data on race have been collected since the first U.S. decennial census in 1790, but it was not until Census 2000 that the census allowed individuals to self-identify with more than one race. The new category, "Two or more races," refers to people who indicate that their heritage is more than one of the six single race categories. These individuals are referred to as the *Two or more races* population, or as persons who reported *more than one race*. Today, they are also commonly referred to as *multiracials*.

According to the U.S. Department of Commerce's Bureau of Census 2000 report, "the U.S. population was 281.4 million on April 1, 2000 and from that total 6.8 million or 2.4 percent identified themselves as more than one race or multiracial" (U.S. Department of Commerce, United States Census 2000, 2001). This Bureau of Census 2000 report was very unique and the first of its type primarily because respondents were given the option of selecting one or more categories to indicate their racial identities.

The Bureau of Census 2000 question on race included not only 15 separate response categories but also 3 areas where respondents could write in a more specific race. The write-in answers and the response categories were combined to create the five standard Office of Management and

Budget race categories plus the U.S. Census Bureau category of "some other race." The six categories were as follows:

- White
- Black or African American
- Asian
- American Indian and Alaska Native
- Native Hawaiian or Other Pacific Islander
- Some other race

Individuals who selected more than one of the six race categories were referred to as the "Two or more races population." For example, the U.S. Census Bureau stated that "respondents who reported they were 'White and American Indian and Alaska Native and Asian' or 'White and Black or African American' were included in the Two or more races category" (U.S. Department of Commerce, United States Census 2000, 2001).

As stated in Chapter 1, the 2000 Census reported that "there are 6.8 million or 2.4 percent individuals as more than one race" (U.S. Department of Commerce, United States Census 2000, 2001). When this racial grouping was further analyzed, an overwhelming majority (93 percent) reported exactly two races, 6 percent reported three races, and 1 percent reported four or more races (2). Table 2.1 shows the number and percentage of respondents to U.S. Census 2000 by number of races reported.

Table 2.1   Total Population by Number of Races Reported, 2000

Number of Races	Number	Percentage of Total Population	Percentage of Total Two or More Races Population
Total population	**281,421,906**	**100.0**	N/A
One race	274,595,678	97.6	N/A
Two or more races	6,826,228	2.4	100.0
Two races	6,368,075	2.3	93.3
Three races	410,285	0.1	6.0
Four races	38,408	–	0.6
Five races	8,637	–	0.1
Six races	823	–	–

– Percentage rounds to 0.0.
N/A: Not applicable.
Source: U.S. Census Bureau, Census 2000 Redistricting Data (Public Law 94-171), Summary File, Table PL1.

Geographic Distribution

A closer examination of the geographical distribution of the U.S. individual citizens in the Two or more races population revealed an interesting pattern. Specifically, the U.S. Bureau of Census reported that "40 percent lived in the West, 27 percent lived in the South, 18 percent lived in the Northeast, and 15 percent lived in the Midwest" (U.S. Department of Commerce, United States Census 2000, 2001).

Since there is always some uncertainty regarding which states belong to which particular region, here is the regional geographic distribution used by the Census Bureau (U.S. Department of Commerce, United States Census 2000, 2001):

- The West Region consists of Alaska, Arizona, California, Colorado, Hawaii, Idaho, Montana, Nevada, New Mexico, Oregon, Utah, Washington and Wyoming.
- The South Region consists of Alabama, Arkansas, Delaware, Florida, Georgia, Kentucky, Louisiana, Maryland, Mississippi, North Carolina, Oklahoma, South Carolina, Tennessee, Texas, Virginia, West Virginia and the District of Columbia.
- The Northeast Region consists of Connecticut, Maine, Massachusetts, New Hampshire, New Jersey, New York, Pennsylvania, Rhode Island, and Vermont.
- The Midwest Region consists of Illinois, Indiana, Iowa, Kansas, Michigan, Minnesota, Missouri, Nebraska, North Dakota, Ohio, South Dakota and Wisconsin.

In the West region of the United States, Alaska and Hawaii have the largest share of people who identify with two or more races. In the continental United States, California and Oklahoma are home to the largest percentage of multiracials (U.S. Department of Commerce, United States Census 2000, 2001).

States

In examining where multiracials live in the United States, the U.S. Bureau of Census reported that "nearly two-thirds of all people who reported more than one race lived in just ten states" (U.S. Department of Commerce, United States Census 2000, 2001). The 10 states with the largest percentage of multiracials in 2000 were California, New York, Texas, Florida, Hawaii, Illinois, New Jersey, Washington, Michigan, and Ohio.

Combined, these states accounted for 64 percent of the total Two or more races.

Upon further analysis, the 2000 U.S. Bureau of Census demographers stated that "three states had Two or more races population greater than 500,000 and they were California (greater than one million), New York (590,000) and Texas (515,000)" (U.S. Department of Commerce, United States Census 2000, 2001). These three states accounted for 40 percent of the total Two or more races population.

The 2000 U.S. Bureau of Census also reported that "states with lower percentages of Two or more races (1.0 percent or less) were Alabama, Maine, Mississippi, South Carolina and West Virginia" (U.S. Department of Commerce, United States Census 2000, 2001: 3). These states were expected to have lower numbers of multiracials.

Counties and Cities

The 2000 U.S. Bureau of Census report also showed similar trends for multiracial populations in counties and cities across the America. Multiracials were found in higher percentages in the West and Southwest counties and cities of the United States (U.S. Department of Commerce, United States Census 2000, 2001).

Age Distribution

The multiracial population is also younger than other racial populations in the United States. Specifically, the U.S. Bureau of Census reported that "42 percent of the population identified themselves as Two or more races and only 25% reported one race" (U.S. Department of Commerce, United States Census 2000, 2001: 9).

Major Themes: U.S. Census 2000

In the federal government, Census 2000 will go down as a major historical turning point as to how all U.S. citizens began to recognize and view the sociocultural and demographic significance of multiracial populations throughout the United States. For the first time ever, the U.S. Bureau of Census changed its survey form to give respondents the option of selecting one or more race categories to indicate their racial identities. In all, the U.S. 2000 Census provided respondents with 15 separate response categories and 3 areas in which respondents could write in a more specific race (U.S. Department of Commerce, United States Census 2000, 2001: 2).

The 6.8 million people who reported *more than one race* in the 2000 Census became a milestone in the data sets of the U.S. Census. That's a remarkable 6.8 million people who were biologically, historically, socially, politically, and culturally ready to identify themselves as multiracial! We might assume the number of multiracials was actually larger than the official tally, because some multiracial individuals do not choose to identify themselves as such, but rather choose to identify with the single race they were raised most exposed to, or feel most like.

For these nearly 7 million multiracials who self-identified as such in 2000, the U.S. Census discovered that there were distinctive patterns of racial, geographic, and age distribution in the United States (American Demographics 2002).

This trend in the U.S. population statistics can no longer be overlooked or underestimated. As the U.S. Census data clearly showed, multiracial populations throughout each region, state, county, and city of the United States have been increasing much more rapidly than demographers had projected.

THE 2010 CENSUS REPORT: CURRENT TRENDS AMONG MULTIRACIALS IN AMERICA

While I was writing this book, the U.S. Bureau of Census 2010 data were in the process of being released to the general public. In the initial phase of reporting the data, U.S. Bureau of Census researchers said that there were very significant new discoveries and trends for this population. For example, Saulny (2011) reviewed the U.S. Bureau of Census 2010 report and stated that "among American children, the multiracial population has increased 50 percent to 4.2 million since 2000, making it the fast growing youth group in the country." The data also revealed that the multiracial population is quite young, and that American Indians and Native Hawaiians and Pacific Islanders are the most likely groups to report being of more than one race, whereas blacks and whites are the least likely to do so (Saulny 2011; U.S. Department of Commerce, United States Census 2000, 2011; Census Scope 2009).

Race

Census 2010 is the first comprehensive assessment of the multiracial population during a 10-year period. With these new data, demographers have recognized some new trends among multiracials. The U.S. Bureau of Census 2010 reported that "of the 57 racial combinations on the census and those who chose more than one race, most chose one of the four most common combinations: 20.4 percent marked black and white; 19.3 percent chose white and 'some other race' " (U.S. Department of Commerce, United States Census 2000, 2011). The third most prevalent combination was Asian and white, followed by American Indian and white. These four combinations accounted for three-fourths of the total mixed race population.

According to the 2010 Census, 308.7 million people resided in the United States on April 1, 2010—which represented an increase of 27.3 million people, or 9.7 percent, between 2000 and 2010. Furthermore, the U.S. Bureau of Census demographers contended that "the vast majority of the growth in the total population came from increases in those who reported their race(s) as something other than White alone and those who reported their ethnicity as Hispanic or Latino" (U.S. Department of Commerce, United States Census 2000, 2011: 3).

In the 2010 Census, approximately 3 percent (9.9 million) of the total population reported themselves as belonging to more than one race. This equates to an increase of 32 percent from 2000 to 2010, making the Two or more races group one of the fastest-growing groups across the decade (U.S. Department of Commerce, United States Census 2000, 2011: 5).

The U.S. Bureau of Census demographers reported that not only were the Asian alone group the fastest-growing racial group during the decade from 2000 to 2010, but their numbers also increased by approximately 43 percent during this decade (U.S. Department of Commerce, United States Census 2000, 2011). Moreover, "the Asian alone population had the second largest numeric change (4.4 million) growing from 10.2 million in 2000 to 14.7 million in 2010" (U.S. Department of Commerce, United States Census 2000, 2011). Owing to this significant increase, the Asian alone population's share of the total population increased the most dramatically over the 10-year period, expanding from approximately 4 percent in 2000 to 5 percent in 2010 (5).

When analyzing other major race group data, the U.S. Bureau of Census demographers acknowledged that the Native Hawaiian and other Pacific Islander alone population also grew significantly between 2000 and 2010, increasing by more than one-third (U.S. Department of Commerce, United States Census 2000, 2011). They reported that "the actual population numbers for this population numbered approximately 398,000 in 2000, rising to 540,013 by 2010 increasing its proportion of the total population from 0.1 percent to 0.2 percent, respectively" (5).

Between 2000 and 2010, the U.S. Bureau of Census demographers noted, the population classified as Some other race alone increased approximately 25 percent (U.S. Department of Commerce, United States Census 2000, 2011). Specifically, the U.S. Bureau of Census data showed that "this population climbed from 15.4 million in 2000 to 19.1 million in 2010 and was approximately six percent of the total population in both decennial census" (5). More than likely, the cause for this growth was probably due to increases in the Hispanic/Latino population.

The two populations that showed the smallest and no percentage growth were the black and white populations. U.S. Bureau of Census demographers noted that "while the Black alone population had the third largest numeric increase in population size over the decade (4.3 million), behind the White alone and Asian alone populations, it grew slower than most other major race groups" (U.S. Department of Commerce, United States Census 2000, 2011). Between 2000 and 2010, the Black alone population exhibited the smallest growth aside from the White alone population, increasing 12 percent. Specifically, the Black population rose from 34.7 million in 2000 to 38.9 million in 2010, making up 12 percent and 13 percent of the total population (5).

Finally, the U.S. Bureau of Census demographers reported that "the only major race group to experience a decrease in its proportion of the total population was the White alone population" (U.S. Department of Commerce, United States Census 2000, 2001). While this group increased the most in terms of raw numbers between 2000 and 2010 (from 211.5 million to 223.6 million), its share of the total population fell from 75 percent in 2000 to 72 percent in 2010 (U.S. Department of Commerce, United States Census 2000, 2011).

Geographic and State Distribution

In the 2010 Census Report, the geographic distribution of those who identified themselves as multiracial was not highlighted in early reports. The 2010 Census Report, however, did point out the "minority" population geographic distribution across the country and indicate that the "minority" population increased from 86.9 million to 111.9 million between 2000 and 2010. These numbers represented growth of 29 percent over the decade.

In some states, the distribution of the multiracial population from the U.S. Census category for minority population was evaluated by demographic centers across the country. According to demographers at the University of Virginia's Weldon Cooper Center for Public Service (2011), four notable themes emerged from their analysis for Virginia:

1. More than 2.9 percent of Virginia residents reported that they belong to two or more of the six race categories counted in the federal census.

2. There was an increase in the multiple-race population from the 2000 Census data.

3. Most multiracial Virginians reported belonging to just two races. Of the biracial Virginians, 29 percent reported being white and black; 28 percent white and Asian; and the remainder other combinations of the six race categories.

4. Multiracial Virginians tend to live in metropolitan areas (University of Virginia 2011: 1).

Major Themes: U.S. Census 2010

The U.S. Bureau of Census 2010 data illustrated that the nation is continuing to change racially and ethnically. During the past 10 years, census data showed that the Hispanic/Latino and Asian American populations have grown the most when compared to other racial and ethnic populations in the United States (U.S. Department of Commerce, United States Census 2000, 2011: 22). The Census 2010 data also showed that one of the fastest-growing populations was people reporting more than one race.

CONCLUSION

The national and local data continue to be collected each decennial, and U.S. Census data continue to show a significant increase in the multiracial and multiethnic populations. According to University of Texas sociology professor Ronald Angel (2011: 1), "The significant increase is not particularly surprising to those who study population trends ... It's just a reflection of the fact that the barriers that separate people are probably not as strong as they were, children are not ashamed to claim that they're multiracial, and for a lot of people, it's a point of pride."

In an article entitled "The Meaning and Measurement of Race in the U.S. Census: Glimpses into the Future," Hirschman, Alba and Farley noted, "when [the] governmental statistical system recognizes that multiple racial ancestry deserves to be part of the record keeping, more people may be willing to acknowledge (or seek information about) mixed ancestry" (2000: 390). Hirschman, Alba, and Farley also contended that the change in record keeping may break down one of the last fears about interracial marriage: the question of where the children will fit in.

These comments from Hirschman, Alba, and Farley (2000), and Angel (2011) were also reflected in the qualitative comments that I collected as part of my study. Specifically, informant #4 stated the following when asked, "Do you think more people in the United States will identify themselves as multiracial each year?":

> Yes, I think this will continue to increase. More and more multiracial people are getting a voice, and are not ashamed to freely express themselves any longer. More are realizing they do not "fit" with just one racial group, and many are realizing this for the first time.

This is a feeling and belief among many multiracials in America today. Their time is now, and they are taking control of their identity, their heritage, and their future regardless of how society chooses to categorize them.

THREE

Struggling with Identity and Place within U.S. Society

INTRODUCTION

Throughout my early childhood years in Ohio, I always knew which racial group society placed me in. In the late 1950s, society categorized individuals like me as "Negro." Later, in the 1960s, society categorized individuals like me as "Black American"; in the early 1970s, society categorized individuals like me as "Afro American"; and then in the 1970s and 1980s, as "African American." Although in each decade society attempted to find the "culturally appropriate label" for multiracials, we were still recognized by society, and within our large racial grouping, as a distinctive racial population physically and often culturally different from the majority.

The most obvious difference between African Americans and Caucasians was skin color. As a darker-complected African American, I could not be mistaken for a member of any other racial group. Moreover, my facial features and hair fell within the typical range of what an African American male looked like. So when someone looked at me, as well as when I looked into the mirror, I and others rightly assumed that I could be classified as an African American.

However, according to my mother, she never saw her children, and herself, as just "African American." She always stressed to us that we had a lot of different races within us, and we needed to appreciate that diverse heritage. That is the major reason why she never agreed with the limited racial categorizations that our society adhered to and implemented.

Yet I often wondered, for those individuals who did not "fit" the typical racial categories, how did they arrive at their own "individual" identity?

Many of my close family members (cousins, nieces, and nephews) and friends at school faced this predicament, and I often wondered what they had to go through mentally. Did it affect their personality, their self-esteem, their aspirations, and their identity? Although times have significantly changed since I grew up in the 1950s through 1970s, I still wonder if those individuals who do not fit neatly within our society's typical racial categories struggle with their identity and place in society.

I posed a question to multiracial people on my survey regarding whether it mattered how one is categorized within a racial and/or ethnic category. Informant #6 stated:

> Yes and no. Yes, because often certain races or ethnic groups are always grouped together. For example, when asked about my race on an application I usually have to identify as Pacific Islander/Asian even though I do not consider myself Asian. Other times it does not matter because I am use to people trying to guess my racial background.

This chapter focuses on multiracials' identity and place in society, and provides a framework to further investigate the multiple issues that many multiracials face throughout their lifetime. Issues that this chapter examines include the following:

- What are the major factors that feed into one's multiracial identity?
- With which racial group or groups will multiracial individuals tend to associate as they go through childhood to adolescence and adulthood?
- How do multiracials overcome the subtle and overt discriminatory practices both from mainstream society and from the specific racial/ethnic groups with whom they associate?
- How do black multiracials and Latino white multiracials differ in their life experiences?

This examination gives us an opportunity to acknowledge and recognize how each multiracial group has differing experiences and circumstances that influences its members' self-identification and place in society.

THE MULTIRACIAL IDENTITY: INFLUENCING FACTORS

Most Americans still perceive that when we speak of multiracials, we are primarily referring to biracial individuals—individuals who have parents of either African American and Caucasian backgrounds. Yet, as we have discovered, multiracials encompass a wide array of mixed heritages, and this diversity is not exclusive to one or two primary races here in the United States. Although much has been written regarding the biracial experiences between Caucasians and African Americans, today we must expand our view and perspectives to examine the multiple experiences and multiple combinations among multiracials so that we can better understand the significant issues that influence their "individual" and "group" identity.

In Maria Root's book *The Multiracial Experience: Racial Borders as the New Frontier (1995)* and particularly in her book chapter entitled "Five Mixed-Race Identities: From Relic to Revolution" in Winters and DeBose's *New Faces in a Changing America* (2003), Root contends that we should use an ecological framework for understanding the multiracial identity today, because it allows us to recognize the multitude of factors that influence a multiracial's self- and group identities. When the ecological model incorporates history, geographical, and gender lenses, identity—both racial and ethnic—will always be in flux because these perspectives are dynamic. The ecological framework for identity development not only explains the different ways in which people come to identify themselves, but also allows for understanding the social, cultural, and familial environments and experiences that shape conventional monoracial identities, racially simultaneous identities, or multiracial identities (Root 2003: 11).

From this ecological model, Root (2003) emphasizes six major factors to consider when examining the multiracial identity: (1) geographical history of race, (2) generation, (3) family influences, (4) gender, (5) community, and (6) individual "personality." When the diversity apparent within these broad categories of influence, even among siblings, is not taken into account, according to Root (2003) attempts to discuss identity choices stay at a very unsophisticated level. Let's briefly review these six major factors.

Geographical Historical Race, Ethnic Relations, and Racial Demographics

Upon reviewing the 2000 and 2010 U.S. Census reports on the major locations among multiracials throughout the United States, it becomes apparent that these persons are neither evenly distributed nor represented by the same mixtures throughout the country. Yet the data definitely indicate that there are substantial increases in multiracial populations in states such as Hawaii, California, Arizona, New Mexico, New York, and Texas. Root

(2003) emphasizes that one of the reasons for the continual growth has to do with more opportunities for interracial contact that come through assimilation and immigration in a post-civil rights era.

Generation

How our society views multiracials—whether positively or negatively— is highly dependent on the beholder's age group. If an individual is a part of the generation that experienced first-hand Jim Crow segregation, anti-Asian sentiments, and denigration of persons of Mexican and Indian heritage, his or her perspective of multiracials will tend to be more negative than positive. Conversely, if an individual is of a younger generation, he or she is more likely to be more favorably disposed toward multiracials. More specifically, in a survey conducted by pollsters operating a *USA Today*/ CNN/Gallup Poll (2001), among respondents in the 18- to 29-year-old group, a majority felt positive about the multiracial future for the country, whereas a majority of those who were 65 years or older held unfavorable attitudes (Root 2003). Thus an individual's age group has an impact on his or her perception of multiracials.

Family Influences

Family influences result from socialization, ethnic markers, and biology. According to Root (2003: 5), "they range from a parent's nativity that affected particular generations of multiracial Asians (e.g., Korean War era and Vietnam War era), given names, languages spoken in the home, phenotype, and sexual orientation." Family influences have also had a tremendous effect on the identity of biracial children whose parents are Caucasian and black.

For example, clinical social worker Dorcas Bowles (1993) stated in her article entitled "Bi-racial Identity: Children Born to African American and White Couples," that she has worked with 10 young adult children of mixed black/white parentage throughout her clinical practice. Bowles found that treatment of each of these young adults was very much related to their denial of part of their ethnicity. Their choice of ethnic identity was related more to societal norms and expectations, which, in part, were transmitted to them by their parents. Each young biracial adult had the developmental task of integrating two ethnic identities and two cultural backgrounds into a positive ethnic identity. Coming to terms with consolidating one's personhood (ethnic identity, sexuality, another round of separation from one's parents) is a task faced by every young adult, but this task is complicated and made more difficult for the biracial young adult given societal attitudes and the need for acceptance by peers, colleagues, and the community at large (Bowles 1993: 422).

Gender

Usually mothers pass on their culture to their children. If the mother is multiracial, she will tend to enculturate her multiracial heritage to her children. However, if the mother does not identify herself as multiracial, there is a lower chance that the children will be identified as multiracial.

For example, Bowles (1993) indicated that in three of her cases in her clinical practice in which the mothers were white and the fathers were black, each of these mothers had told their daughters, in different ways, that because they were females, their identification should be with the mother, who was white. Two of the mothers had expressed that being white would make for "an easier time in the world" for their daughters. In each of these three cases, there were feelings of shame by the daughters at denying a part of who they were—feelings of isolation, of feeling false and not being real. In addition to feelings of shame, all three young women experienced varying levels of anxiety, which seemed related to a felt sense of danger given the discrepancy between their core biracial self and the coercion by family or society to own only one part of the experience of the self (420).

Community

Another key factor in Root's (2003) ecological model is the community. The community in which one grows up reflects, to varying degrees, values, expectations, and a home. These can be one's actual home, neighborhood, school, workplace, place of worship, and places of recreation. Usually parents and older siblings negotiate a child's identity with each of these communities.

Root (2003) contended that "there are two predictable situations in which the community has a direct influence on the multiracial individual's life"—namely, dating and moving. In dating, the community will have some influence on the degree to which interracial dating is accepted and which groups are viewed as viable partners. The second potentially difficult transition point comes when multiracial people leave their home communities and need to renegotiate their identity on their own.

Personality

The final factor in Root's (2003) ecological model is personality. The degree to which one has outstanding talents or social skills affects how he or she negotiates identity in the presence of opposition or authenticity. For example, if one is an outstanding athlete, musician, or student, he or she may belong to a subculture or group based on these skills. Race may often have background salience. If one is very "thin skinned," he or she may be acutely sensitive to slights. Race may become the foreground in this scenario (13).

The Multiracial Identity: The Result

According to Root (2003), the six major factors influencing one's identity may combine to result in any of the following choices relative to multiracial identity:

1. Accept the identity society assigns.
2. Choose a single identity.
3. Choose a mixed identity.
4. Choose a new race identity
5. Choose a white identity.

Identity is dynamic and informed by one's life experiences in a historical context. These possible multiracial identities are the result of the interplay of one's generation, geographic region, gender, community, and personality. Because of America's constant struggle with the issues of race and race relations, we will continue to witness a new array of factors influencing individuals' multiracial identities.

MULTIRACIAL IDENTITIES: EXAMPLES

As we documented in Chapter 2, U.S. Bureau of Census data show that America's multiracial population is primarily clustered in the western region of the United States, with nearly two-thirds of multiracials residing in just 10 states. In California, 1.6 million people identified themselves as multiracial, accounting for 4.7 percent of the state's population, or one in every 21 Californians (Lee and Bean 2007).

Wide variations in rates of multiracial reporting also occur across groups. Lee and Bean (2007) report that "12 percent of Asians and 16 percent of 'Other' Americans (i.e., Latinos) identified multiracially, yet only 4 percent of the black population did" (Tafoya et al. 2005). The rate of multiracial reporting among blacks is much lower compared to other groups, even after controlling for differences in age, education, nativity, gender, and region of the United States (Tafoya et al. 2005). Tafoya et al. (2005) emphasize that while the U.S. Census estimates that at least three-fourths of all blacks in the United States are ancestrally multiracial, slightly more than 4 percent choose to identify as such, indicating that most black Americans do not depend strictly on their genealogy to identify themselves, but instead rely on the social and cultural construction of racial boundaries. Overall, the rate of multiracial reporting is three and four times higher among Asians and Latinos, respectively, than among blacks, suggesting that the historical absence of the constraining "one-drop rule" for the former groups may provide more opportunity in exercising discretion in the selection of racial/ethnic identities (Harris and Sim 2002; Xie and Goyette 1997).

Multiracial Blacks' Identity

Lee and Bean's (2007) examination of both the 2000 U.S. Census and of 46 in-depth interviews of multiracial adults in southern and northern California found that multiracial blacks were less likely to identify multiracially compared to their Asian and Latino counterparts primarily because of their outsiders' perspective, which powerfully influences one's choice of identities. In other words, because other races identify them as black, many times multiracial blacks are less likely to identify themselves as multiracial. For example, when Lee and Bean asked a 33-year-old woman born to a white mother and a black father why she chose to identify as black on the census form, she explained:

> I feel if somebody is going to look at me, they're not going to think I'm white so I put black ... I mean, I know that I'm mixed, but if it were to come up, and it were to be a choice, one or other, I would say I'm black. (Lee and Bean 2007: 573)

Other multiracial adults with one black and one white parent stated similar sentiments; that is, while they recognized the racial mixture in their backgrounds, they chose to identify as black. A 26-year-old stated, "I think the main reason I identify as black is if someone looks at me, I don't really necessarily look white." Lee and Bean (2007: 574) contend that "if one looks black, one cannot be white." So powerful is the force of outsiders' perspective that the 26-year-old individual chose to identify his son, whom he conceived with a white woman, as black rather than as multiracial or white (574). Other black multiracials (e.g., black-Asian and black-Latino multiracials) similarly feel that people often see and identify them as black and fail to acknowledge their Asian or Latino ancestries.

In another study on racial identity, Kerwin et al. (1993) conducted a qualitative study consisting of semi-structured interviews among nine black/white biracial children and their parents (a total of six interracial families). These interviews were audiotaped and conducted individually in the homes of the participants and lasted from one hour to more than two hours. Kerwin et al. (1993) found that the majority of participant children, adolescents, and adults demonstrated sensitivity to the views, cultures, and values of both the black and white communities.

Topics covered in the parent interview guide in Kerwin et al.'s (1993) study included family's identify, use/nonuse of an interracial label, racial awareness of child or children, dual socialization, family's coping skills, developmental issues and problems, sociocultural factors, and the role of schools. For the children's interviews, topics covered included self-identity, use/nonuse of an interracial label, racial awareness, dual socialization, and the family's coping skills.

A major theme emerged from the parent interviews concerning the use or nonuse of racially identifying labels for the family and the child or children. Specifically, parents' feelings tended to be strongly expressed with regard to decrying society's demand that individuals label themselves racially/ethnically. Kerwin et al. (1993) noted that a white father stated, "Interracial is only a problem because race is a problem." A number of parents voiced their distress about needing to fill out census forms requiring racial/ethnic designations for their children.

Another perspective expressed in the interviews was that not having a label is the core problem in identity formation for biracial children. One black father stated that not having a term implies that his daughters will have to choose one race over the other. Kerwin et al. (1993) contend that the father feared that this process would lead to questioning about which race is "better."

Additionally, a number of parents recalled having responded to their child's inquiry about his or her racial status. Some parents told their child that he or she was "both black and white" or "[you] have a little of daddy and a little of mommy." Among the parents, Kerwin et al. (1993) suggest, preferred labels for the families included "interracial," "mixed," "black," "black and white," and "bicultural."

Finally, Kerwin et al. (1993) note that in families in which the use of a label had not been brought up by a child's spontaneous question or by the parents themselves, children often created their own label/category. According to their parents, these children referred to themselves as "mixed," "tan," "brown," or "coffee and cream." In some cases, the parent thought that the child had heard the term outside the home, whereas in other cases it seemed to be a description based on the child's observance of his or her own skin color (225).

Another major theme that emerged from the parents' interviews was the preparation for anticipated discrimination. Many participant parents expressed concern about racial discrimination, which they anticipated for their child or children. Within the second emergent theme, Kerwin et al. (1993) note that a dichotomy surfaced as to how some of the black parents and some of the white parents viewed this issue: some families sought to actively prepare their child or children to deal with prejudice, whereas others attempted to protect them from exposure to situations involving potential prejudice (225).

Kerwin et al. (1993) also mention another interesting perspective that emerged from the parent interviews—namely, that biracial individuals are uniquely prepared to deal with issues related to differences between people, cultures, and so forth, as well as societal discrimination. One of their informants, a black mother, stated, "If you're only exposed to one thing, you may feel very comfortable with that one thing but you just never really learn to deal with the other" (225).

The final major theme from the parents' interviews was location of the family. Kerwin et al. (1993) found that many of the parents discussed the choice of where to bring up their child or children as a central issue for the family. These parents acknowledged the primary importance of factors such as racial composition of the neighborhood and perceived "openness" of the area to interracial families.

For example, "a black mother of two felt that if her family were living in a monoracial neighborhood, they would need to spend more time dealing with racial issues" (Kerwin et al. 1993). This woman noted that "We haven't had to face the kind of stuff that people would have to face in other places" (225).

The other portion of Kerwin et al.'s (1993) study involved children. From the child interviews, the researchers discovered several emergent themes such as use/nonuse of racial ethnic labels, location of the family, preparation for anticipate discrimination, self-description, and racial awareness.

When asked whether they had felt pressured to choose one color over another as their primary identification, the four eldest child respondents could recall such situations. These adolescents spoke of peer pressures to choose a group of friends according to race. Kerwin et al. (1993) highlighted the comments from a 13-year-old: "Like, at school the kids section

themselves. The black kids stay together and the white kids stay together."
This 13-year-old further stated some of the mixed kids went with the black
kids and some went with the white kids. In particular, she said, "There
isn't a mixed group" (226).

The children participating in the study were asked to describe themselves in terms of their physical appearance; they were asked what they
would say to someone who had never seen them who was to meet them
at a given place. In addressing this issue, Kerwin et al. (1993) mention
comments from a 5-year-old and a 7-year-old, both of whom had some
difficulty describing themselves, yet both of whom were also very
descriptive when given more opportunity.

Finally, Kerwin et al. (1993) acknowledged another theme among the
children—racial awareness. They found that the majority of participants
did not recall a specific time or incident when they first became aware of
racial categories, racial differences, or both. Younger children, especially,
spoke of their awareness in a general way. Kerwin et al. (1993) note that
their oldest respondent (age 16) demonstrated insight into how his development of racial awareness might have been linked to this initial experience with racial discrimination. Specifically, the 16-year-old stated, "I
didn't even notice the difference until, you know, people started talking
about it and it became an issue all of a sudden. It wasn't an issue to me"
(227).

In conclusion, Kerwin et al. (1993) contend that the major findings from
the analysis of their interviews with parents and children often ran counter
to the problems that historically have been conjectured for this population.
First, for all of the respondent children and adolescents, there was no great
sense of perceiving themselves as marginal in two cultures. Moreover,
parents seemed to have a secure sense of their own racial identity. Additionally, none of the participant families reported alienation from their
extended families as a result of their interracial marriage. Finally, many
of the families reported an openness to talking about racial issues within
their families; according to Kerwin et al. (1993), this is one major research
area that needs to be further explored to find out more about the real-life
issues associated with interracial couples and their children.

Multiracial Asian-Whites' and Latino-Whites' Identity

To better understand the specific racial identity issues among multiracial Asian-whites and Latino whites, Lee and Bean (2007), in an article
entitled "Reinventing the Color Line: Immigration and America's New
Racial/Ethnic Divide," highlighted the difference between black

multiracials versus Asian-white and Latino-white multiracials. These authors conducted 30 in-depth interviews with Asian-white and Latino-white multiracials. Lee and Bean (2007) found that multiracial Asian-whites and Latino-whites felt that they have much more opportunity to choose among different racial options, including multiracial and white identities. Some chose to identify as half-Latino, half-Asian, and half-white, and others did not ascribe to a monoracial Latino or Asian identity. Lee and Bean (2007) also note that unlike black-white multiracials, Latino-white and Asian-white multiracials are often identified as white, which affects the way they see themselves.

For example, Lee and Bean (2007) stated that some of the multiracial Latino-whites felt that they look "white" without a hint of Latino ethnicity. One informant stated, "I feel like I'm white with a hint of Mexican. I do have a Mexican background, family, and heritage yet I identify with being white more just because that's the way I look" (574).

Lee and Bean (2007) also interviewed an Asian-white multiracial man who expressed the view that race will not affect his life chances; he also does not believe that race matters much for anyone who is "really good" at what they do. Specifically, this informant said, "Well, at least in the U.S. you can be very successful, so I don't think how I look on the outside affects it. I don't see limits" (577).

In general, Lee and Bean (2007) contend that their sample of Asian-white multiracials treated their Asian ethnicities as cultures to be acquired and factors that will make their lives more interesting. More importantly, the authors stress that these multiracials are accepted by others, signaling the voluntary and optional nature of Asian ethnicity for the multiracial respondents (578).

CONCLUSION

This chapter focused on multiracials' identity and place in society and provided a framework to further investigate the multiple issues that many multiracials face throughout their lifetime. The discussion answered the following questions:

- What are the major factors that feed into one's multiracial identity?
- With which racial group or groups will multiracial individuals tend to associate as they go through childhood to adolescence and adulthood?
- How do multiracials overcome the subtle and overt discriminatory practices both from mainstream society and from the specific racial/ethnic groups with whom they associate?

The comments from informant #5 supported the qualitative results from the documented research studies in this chapter. For example, when asked the question, "How would you describe a multiracial person?" informant #5 responded as follows:

Well, I describe myself as multiracial or biracial to be specific for people. I am clearly a product of two people of different races, so it makes sense to describe myself that way. I have found that some people don't recognize that I am biracial and assume I am some shade of either white or black—which I find pretty amusing at times. I think of a multiracial person as someone who has parents of different races, but I think it also applies to people whose parents are multiracial. But then again, how many multiracial generations does one have to trace back before the description is "diluted" out? If that were the case, then plenty of Americans are multiracial and should be aware, right? I think the problem is that people of multiracial descent who don't necessarily look like it, or feel like it, will be the hardest group to persuade. They are probably less likely to identify as multiracial if they are already comfortable identifying as only one race.

In a country that applauds its diversity and "melting pot" history, one would think that today's U.S. citizens would not have to struggle with their identity and place in society, but unfortunately a majority of multiracials have to deal with this issue every day. The results from several research scholars and their studies, along with my key informant's comments, show that multiracials not only experience a unique set of racial identity issues throughout their lifetime, but also learn how to adapt to society's racial discriminatory practices.

PART II

Background Issues

FOUR

The Cultural History of Multiracialism in America

INTRODUCTION

The concepts of race and race relations still evoke all types of sensitive, personal, social, familial, and cultural emotions. These issues become particularly heightened when individuals of different races develop interracial relationships that may result in an offspring between the two. When this occurs, there is usually some type of reaction, whether positive or negative, from close family members, friends, associates, community members, and society in general.

Since 1967, when the U.S. Supreme Court ruled bans on interracial cohabitation and marriage are unconstitutional, interracial relationships in the country have increased sharply. As of 2005, rates of interracial marriages were 10 times greater among whites, blacks, and Hispanics than in the 1960s. Even among Asian Americans, 12 percent of the men and 25 percent of the women married non-Asians (Alderman 2007: 12).

In spite of these increases, interracial marriage occurs less frequently than same-race unions. In 2002, interracial marriages accounted for only 2.9 percent of all marriages in the United States, and only 5.7 percent of Americans involved in serious romantic relationships were dating or living with partners of a different race. In a study conducted by Cornell University, researchers found that while youths were more likely than their elders to be involved in interracial relationships overall, they nevertheless remained relatively secretive about them, apparently fearing the disapproval of their families or their peers. Young women were also reportedly more likely to hide pregnancies resulting from intercourse with a partner of a different race. Thus the relative infrequency of mixed-race unions and the need for secrecy or discretion described by many who date interracially suggest that while attitudes may be changing, a cultural stigma is still associated with such relationships (Alderman 2007: 12).

Why do members of our society feel this way in 2013? Why are we still amazed when people of all types of ethnic and racial backgrounds decide to have interracial relationships? The answer lies in U.S. history—a history that many would love to forget.

THE BEGINNINGS OF INTERRACIAL RELATIONSHIPS IN AMERICA

From an anthropological perspective, human populations have always been successful in interbreeding and reproducing offspring who can in turn interbreed. From one continent to another, and from one earlier time period to another, human populations have been very successful in increasing their numbers despite the uncertainty of their immediate natural environments and other populations. Whether interbreeding takes place among a population similar in physical attributes or among people with different physical attributes, human populations have been a highly adaptable species (Molnar 1975).

Unfortunately, over time, as human populations interacted with other types of human populations that may have had different physical attributes, categories used for "typing" different human populations became popular. Thus we can see the term *race* is a historical artifact from an archaic biology. These categories of "typing" human populations also became the beginnings of racial categorizations.

As Europeans fanned out across the globe during the age of exploration, the elites of the societies found unparalleled opportunities for the accumulation of wealth and power (Murphy 2001). In many cases, however, these opportunities were only available through the destruction of local societies in North and South America, the Caribbean, Africa, Asia, and the Pacific Islands. In other cases, local indigenous populations were subjugated and recruited into social, economic, and political systems that placed them in the lowest and least privileged classes of the newly emerging colonial social structures (Murphy 2001).

As Murphy (2001: 3) explains, "By the time the American colonies traversed the road of separation from English rule, the concept of race with its implications of institutionalized superiority and inferiority was well embedded in the consciousness, and the economy, of the emerging body politic." The nation's founders struggled to reconcile the concepts of liberty, equality, slavery, and their own economic self-interest. Perhaps they were torn, and perhaps they agonized over the issues, but the union they formed retained slavery for several more generations and culminated in the most costly, tragic, and divisive crisis in American history (Murphy 2001: 3).

Murphy states, "Although the Civil War freed slaves in the United States, it could not eradicate racial divisions nor the attitudes and beliefs that they engendered. Nor was racial discrimination in America confined to the African American population" (3). Native Americans suffered terribly as the country engaged in the westward expansion that many white Americans considered the Unites States' "manifest destiny." Chinese and other Asian people were the target of many discriminatory laws. Even immigrants of European backgrounds commonly suffered discriminatory practices based on their racial backgrounds (Murphy 2001: 3).

With time and the passing of generations, speech accents disappeared and European immigrants gradually became more acceptable to the established white Anglo-Saxon Protestant majority. As American-born offspring of formerly despised European immigrant groups replaced their parents in the population, discrimination against them decreased and many experienced upward social mobility (Murphy 2001: 3–4).

Many researchers believe that the African American population experienced a similar pattern of discrimination and gradual acceptance; even so, because of their skin color and other physical attributes (e.g., hair, eyes, nose, lips, and body type), their discrimination was far more severe and pervasive. For example, an African American who was darker complected was often perceived as less intelligent, less attractive, and less desired than African Americans with lighter skin. Therefore, these darker-complected African Americans received fewer opportunities throughout their lives, ensuring that they maintained at a lower social economic standing than their lighter-complected counterparts.

MIXED-RACE CHILDREN

Mulattos

Historically, the term *mulatto* was used to refer to a person with one white parent and one black parent or, more broadly, a person of mixed black and white ancestry (Winters and DeBose 2003). As Winters and DeBose note, "the term 'mulatto' was also used to refer to the offspring of whites who intermarried with South Asian indentured servants brought over to the British American colonies by the East India Company" (43). In 1680, a typical person referred to as mulatto was a Eurasian daughter born to a South Asian father and Irish mother in Maryland and later sold into slavery. Although still in use, in the last half of the 21st century the term "mulatto" was not used as often and was considered culturally insensitive by some in the United States.

With the concept and the sociopolitical system firmly established around the rules of *race* and *racial discrimination* at the early beginnings of the United States, interracial relationships had to adhere to the nation's law of the land at this point in U.S. history. That law of the land stipulated that people of different races—particularly whites and blacks—were not to have any intimate relations that might potentially result in offspring of the pair. Although in the pre-Civil War South, sexual liaisons between white men and African American women were not uncommon, the opposite was true for black men with white women. Sexual intimacy and interracial relationship between a black man and a white woman was unthinkable and forbidden both before and after the Civil War. Black men were targets of some of the cruelest torture and murder ever known in American history in the period between the 1870s and the 1940s, which their abuse often triggered by accusations of sexual interest in white women (Murphy 2001: 40).

Amalgamation was the initial term used to describe sexual reproduction —within or outside the context of marriage—involving individuals who were presumed to belong to distinct "races," especially those sociologically and biologically designated as "black" or "white." As explained by Ifekwunigwe (2004), with the publication of *Miscegenation: The Theory of the Blending of the Races Applied to the American White and Negro* in 1864, David Goodman Croly introduced the word "miscegenation," which he thought sounded more scientific than "amalgamation." He combined two Latin words, *miscere* ("to mix") and *genus* ("race"), to create *miscegenation* (10).

"Black" and "white" miscegenation dates back to the 16th century and the beginning of the trans-Atlantic slave trade, wherein West Africans were forcibly removed from their homelands and sold as chattel slaves to work on plantations in the southern United States, the Caribbean, and Brazil. In societies whose economies were originally dependent on the exploitation of "non-white" slaves, miscegenation between slave women and their slave masters contributed to the viability of the labor force (Ifekwunigwe 2004: 10).

In 1619, 20 African slaves were purchased in Virginia and used to cultivate the tobacco crop. These early slaves were set to work side by side with white European indentured servants. Children of mixed race were born soon thereafter. The fathers of some these children were white slave traders in Africa and seaman from the Middle Passage, but miscegenation also occurred frequently within the combined slave and indentured-servant laboring class (Zack 1993: 78).

Attempting to reduce the number of mixed-race children, in 1662 Virginia enacted the first law prohibiting interracial marriage. Although the most frequent interracial sex was between white men and black women, the children of these unions were not relegated to their fathers in the tradition of British patriarchy but rather were given the status of their mothers. The mixed-race children of white women were not slaves, but they were often bound to indentured servitude well into their adult years. The white mothers of such children, who had their own periods of servitude extended, were subject to fines and other legal penalties. For example, in 1691, Virginia enacted a law requiring that any free white woman bearing a mulatto child had to pay a fine within 30 days or face indentured servitude for 5 years for herself and 30 years for her child. The child was to be sold as a servant (Zack 1993: 79).

In 1705, the Virginia assembly decreed that any minister who married a racially mixed couple had to pay a fine of 10,000 pounds of tobacco. Eventually it became illegal for mulattoes to marry blacks in Virginia. The states of Maryland and Pennsylvania had stricter penalties against interracial unions and the resulting mulatto children (Zack 1993: 79).

During the period from 1705 to 1725, most of the colonies passed laws similar to those in Virginia, Maryland, and Pennsylvania. However, despite this proscriptive legislation, it has been estimated that by the time of the American Revolution there were between 60,000 and 120,000 people of mixed black and white race in the American colonies. The official U.S. census counted the total black population as 757,000 in 1790, although there was no official count of mixed-raced individuals until 1850, when it was estimated that they represented approximately 3 percent of the minority population (Zack 1993: 79).

By the 1850s, the mixed-race population dramatically increased in numbers in all the states, but their treatment and acceptance varied from state to state. Zack (1993) states in her book, *Race and Mixed Race*, that in the upper South approximately 37 percent of all mulattoes were free and made up 35 percent of the total free Negro population. In Georgia, for example, free mulattoes had all the rights of whites, except for voting and sitting in the assembly. Throughout the lower South, free mulattoes tended to be recognized by whites as an intermediate caste between whites and blacks, perhaps because there were fewer whites in proportion to black slaves in the lower South.

In Louisiana and South Carolina, many free mulattoes were prosperous: they owned both land and slaves, accumulated wealth, and were successful artisans, tradespeople, professionals, and artists. During the entire period of slavery in South Carolina, there was no law against racial intermarriage. In the upper South, free mulattoes were associated with their lower-class white colonial forebears, and they tended to be marginalized both economically and legally (Zack 1993: 81).

Between 1850 and 1915, race relations changed significantly in America. As Williamson (1980) notes in *New People: Miscegenation and Mulattoes in the United States*, this was a period in which America evolved from a stringent slave paradigm of race relations. The transformation in race relations was tied to the emergence of the Industrial Revolution. In the 17th and 18th centuries, the American South had developed plantation slavery to contribute significant quantities of tobacco, rice, and sugar to world commerce. Early in the 19th century, it turned the vast productive power of plantation slavery to supplying most of the world's cotton (Williamson 1980: 61).

In 1850, African Americans were integral to the Industrial Revolution through the institution of slavery. In 1915, they were excluded from direct and organized participation in the Industrial Revolution by institutions of segregation, disfranchisement, and proscription. Thus, in both slavery and freedom, African Americans were steadily and firmly excluded from enjoying an appreciable share of the benefits of industrialization (Williamson 1980: 62).

During this same period, the position of mulattoes and the attitudes held by and about mulattoes were an index to the changeover in race relations. In essence, particularly in the lower South of the United States, the dominant white society moved from semi-acceptance of free mulattoes to outright rejection of these individuals. Williamson (1980: 62) states that "as mulatto communities continue to grow, they experienced more stringent rules against them in the form of laws or of social pressures." Eventually, more and more of the mulatto elite class gave up white alliances and picked up black alliances. This transformation increased in the Civil War, took firm hold during the critical year 1865, and continued throughout Reconstruction, the post-Reconstruction period, and into the 20th century. By the two decades between 1905 and 1925, mulattoes and the mulatto elite had allied themselves totally with the black world (Williamson 1980: 62).

Williamson (1980) also notes that the mulatto elite were strikingly effective in uniting themselves with the black masses and black leadership. Southern-bred black leaders, naturally enough, tended to be ex-slaves from the "black belts," and they represented the interests of ex-slaves. What their constituents most wanted was economic opportunity. In an agrarian society, this desire translated primarily into access to the land and its produce. Mulattoes, in contrast, were more interested in full admission to American society. Thus they stressed integration in all public facilities, from the schools through the common carriers to libraries, the theater, and even the opera. Mulatto and black leaders exhibited a ready ability to mediate their differences and join together in the pursuit of their goals. In terms of legislation, they quickly proved successful in achieving their collective goals (Williamson 1980: 81).

During this changeover of race relations, the number of mulattoes had grown in both absolute and relative terms. The 1850 census counted 406,000 mulattoes among 3,639,000 Negroes. In 1910, it counted 2,051,000 mulattoes in a total Negro population of 9,828,000. In 1850, mulattoes accounted for 11.2 percent of the total Negro population; in 1910, they represented 20.9 percent of the total. According to Williamson (1980), these figures represented only mulattoes whose mixed ancestry was visible to the census takers. Officials of the census estimated that actually some three-fourths of the Negro population in America were mixed race in some degree at this time (63).

In general, although mulattoes were identified, acknowledged, and categorized as a distinguishable racial population separate from the black population by the U.S. census, they were still treated by many Americans as though they were black. Thus, in the white world as well as in the mulattos' world, they were considered black.

The One-Drop Rule

The *one-drop rule* is a societal and cultural rule that significantly changed racial categories and the way in which Americans thought about race, particularly as it related to African Americans. The basic premise behind the one drop is just that: one drop of blood from a particular ancestor (black) will cause a person to be a part of that group. Thus, most supporters of this rule contended that a person with one drop of black blood was, in fact, black.

The "one-drop rule" is similar to the term "hypodescent," meaning that Americans of African physical appearance are considered black, even if their African admixture is less than 50 percent of their total genetic heritage (Harris 1964). Developed by anthropologist Marvin Harris (1964), the concept of hypodescent contends that there are always some physical signs of an individual's blackness regardless of his or her admixture. Some scholars and researchers say that such heritage is revealed in the color of the half-moons at the base of the thumbnails, or in the shape of the heel, or in blue or purple marks at specific locations on the body.

To them, the "one-drop rule" is the belief that no matter how diluted African blood may be, a residue of visible evidence will always remain as a legacy, generation after generation (Harris 1964).

The "one-drop rule" can also mean "invisible blackness." Sweet (2005: 268) states that "this means that someone who appears European is considered Black anyway, presumably due to having some distant intangible Black ancestry." Furthermore, the one-drop rule's contention of invisible blackness happens only in the United States (Sweet 2005: 269).

In Sweet's (2005) book, *Legal History of the Color Line: The Notion of Invisible Darkness*, five major areas of data are cited to illustrate why the one-drop rule of invisible blackness developed in the North between 1830 and 1840: (1) a bidirectional strategy, (2) journals and diaries, (3) literature and drama, (4) court cases, and (5) graphs and charts. In general, Sweet suggests that "the origin of the one-drop rule in the 1830s helped to ensure that blacks could not enter the white world and that whites would be ostracized if they claimed to have any African American heritage since the races lived in parallel, but unequal social statuses" (11). At the same time, the one-drop rule was reinforced and encouraged by African American ethnic leaders seeking to strengthen group loyalties and to maintain their numbers.

Mixed Bloods

As early as the 1500s, the terms *mixed blood*, *half-breed*, and *breed* appeared in historical records to describe the descendants of Indians and the newcomers to the American continent (Baird-Olson 2003). The label "mixed blood" is used most often, given its widespread lay usage. Yet a number of other labels have been used at times as synonyms for all of the various ethnic/national combinations of the descendants of European American "sanctified" unions with American Indians, non-"sanctified" relationships between Indians and non-Indians, and sexual assaults against Indian women by non-Indian males (Baird-Olson 2003: 196).

The fate of the offspring of widespread First Nation miscegenation has been a matter of concern since the colonizers of the 1400s and 1500s came into the lands of the indigenous peoples of the Northeast, Southeast, and Southwest. As Baird-Olson (2003) states in her book chapter entitled "Colonization, Cultural Imperialism, and the Social Construction of American Indian Mixed-Blood Identity," initially, "although both First Nations and Europeans sought political marriages to protect economic and political interests, the invaders and colonizers racialized ideologies created a social issue: What would be the fate of 'mixed-blood' offspring (195) ?"

By the 1860s, American Indians were actually recorded independently on the general U.S. census. According to the U.S. Census Bureau, the average degree of mixed blood among Americans Indians fell between 35 percent and 45 percent. In 1880, "Indian Division" schedules recorded whether respondents were "of full-blood" or whether they embodied "mixture" with whites, blacks, mulattoes, or another tribe (U.S. Census Bureau 1973). In 1910, fractions of Indian, white, and Negro blood were recorded. The U.S. Census Bureau (1973) reported that while "census takers changed to a simple full-blooded/mixed blood dichotomy in 1930, the 1950 census reintroduced the blood quantum construct with the category 'degree of Indian blood' and its response options: 'full blood,' 'half to full,' 'quarter to half,' and 'less than ¼'."

According to U.S. Census data from 1910 to 1950, mixed bloods totaled approximately 94,000 (35% of the total Indian population) in 1910, and their number increased to approximately 137,000 (40% of the total Indian population) in 1950. It is obvious from the census numbers and criteria for mixed bloods that the percentage of mixed bloods dramatically increased during the 40-year period.

Morning (2003) notes that Census officials' definitions of mixed-race people of American Indian origin differed from their definitions concerning mulattoes, in that the former depended upon a range of social, cultural, situational, and behavioral factors. Although Indian blood percentage would be evaluated, the social status of the individual in question remained salient, as powerfully stated by the 1930 census's introduction of the idea of identifying those Indians who were "accepted in the community" as such (U.S. Census Bureau 1973:1). This phrasing, which remained on the census through 1960, sanctioned the exceptional cases in which people of mixed-race ancestry could be assigned to the higher status rather than the lower status of the two racial groups with which they were identified. In other words, individuals of white and Indian origin could be identified as white if their communities recognized them as such, and those of Indian and black origin could be recorded as Indian. In contrast, mulattoes were given no such option; no amount of community recognition could legitimate the transformation from black to white (Morning 2003: 46).

Mestizo

Mestizo is a term traditionally used in Latin America and Spain for people of mixed European and Native American heritage or descent (Winters and DeBose 2003). In the early colonial period, a *mestizo* (*mestiza* for a female) was a child born to Indian and Spanish or Portuguese parents. Typically, the father was Spanish or Portuguese and the mother was Indian, reflecting both the demographics of the early colonial period, where there were far fewer European women in the Americas, and the socially accepted patterns of marriage, concubinage, and sexual relations between members of different racial groups (Sanabria 2007: 111).

In his book, *The Anthropology of Latin America and the Caribbean*, Harry Sanabria (2007: 111) states that, "as unions between Spanish/Portuguese men and Indian or African women produced large numbers of children of mixed ancestry, the categories of *Mestizo* and Mulatto, respectively, came to reflect the emerging racial diversity." Over time, however, racial classification became increasingly complex, as generations of mixing led to multiple intermediate categories in places such as Brazil, Mexico, and Cuba.

As the years passed and intermixing continued, it became more difficult to readily distinguish members of different categories based on physical appearance alone. In Brazil, for example, researchers have compiled a list of 134 physical types based on skin color and other physical characteristics (Sanabria 2007: 112). Sanabria (2007) emphasizes not only that these different categories highlight the remarkable complexity of racial classifications in Brazil, but also that these categories are cultural and not biological classifications. This is true for several reasons.

First, the simple recognition that systems of racial classifications differ from society to society points to the social construction of racial difference. Second, the means by which racial categories are recognized and the meanings attached to these categories change over time and in different contexts. Third, racial classifications and identities are rational and, therefore, emerge and are transformed in the course of social interaction. Finally, the markers of racial difference after the early colonial period are as much cultural as they are physical; therefore, one's identification as a *mestizo*, for example, is as much recognition of differences in dress, language, and occupation as it is a comment on the phenotypic characteristics of that individual (Sanabria 2007: 113).

Over time, as *mestizos* moved into mainstream American society, they became doubly mixed, doubly *mestizo*. Velazco Y Trianosky explains:

> We are mixed for the second time by culture, through our encounter with the dominant culture in this new land. We are mixed for the second time by race, as we intermingle with our new Anglo-European cousins. Thus, we become Puerto Rican Americans, Mexican Americans and Cuban Americans. (Velazco Y Trianosky 2003: 177)

Amerasians

Amerasian refers to a person born in Asia, to a U.S. military father and an Asian mother. According to the Amerasian Foundation (AF) and Amerasian Family Finder (AFF), "Amerasian" is defined as any person who was fathered by a citizen of the United States (an American serviceman), American expatriate, or U.S. government employee (regular or contract) and whose mother is, or was, an Asian national (2011).

The term "Amerasian" is also applied to half-Japanese children fathered by U.S. servicemen in Japan on the island of Okinawa, to children of Filipinos and American rulers during the U.S. colonial period of the Philippines, and to the children of Thais and U.S. soldiers during World War II and the Vietnam War. Since 1898, when the United States first colonized the Philippines, there have been Amerasians (Nimmons 2011).

Hapa Haole

In the Hawaiian language, *hapa* is defined as follows: portion, fragment, part, fraction, installment; to be partial, less (Winters and DeBose 2003). The term *hapa haole*, meaning "half-Caucasian," is used to describe those persons who are half-Asian of Chinese, Japanese, Korean or Filipino ancestry and half-Caucasian. On the islands, those individuals mixed with Asian, Polynesian, and European heritage are most often described as cosmopolitan or local (Nimmons 2011: 48).

Moreover, the term *hapa* can be used in conjunction with other Hawaiian racial and ethnic descriptors to specify a particular racial or ethnic mixture. Some examples follow:

- *Hapa haole* (part Caucasian/white)
- *Hapa kanaka* (part Native Hawaiian)
- *Hapa popolo* (part African/black)
- *Hapa kepani* (part Japanese); the term *hapanese* is also used
- *Hapa pilipino* (part Filipino)
- *Hapa pake* (part Chinese)
- *Hapa kolea* (part Korean)
- *Hapa kamoa* (part Samoan)
- *Hapa sepania* (part Spanish)
- *Hapa pukiki* (part Portuguese/white)

Historically, it is believed that the Hawaiian Islands were first populated by the Polynesians from the Marquesas and Tahiti somewhere between

300 and 500 CE (Nimmons 2011: 47). Centuries later, Europeans arrived to the islands around 1778, with the voyages of British explorer James Cook. The Hawaiian Islands soon became a convenient location for ships to stop and a source for supplies for traders and whalers.

The next major groups to migrate significantly to Hawaii were the Chinese and Japanese. Nimmons (2011: 47) notes that "Chinese workers settled upon Hawaiian shores in 1789 followed by the first legal Japanese immigrants arriving in 1885 also as contract laborers for the pineapple and sugar cane plantations." Shortly afterward, Puerto Rican immigrants entered Hawaii after a natural catastrophe wiped out the fertile lands of Puerto Rico. Next, two waves of Korean immigration occurred, first between 1903 and 1924 and again around 1965.

Other groups of ethnicities also immigrated to the Hawaiian Islands, such as Samoans, Mormons, Fijians, Gilbert Islanders, Norwegians, Spaniards, Germans, and Russians (Nimmons 2011). Filipino immigrants also traveled to Hawaii during the 1840s during the push for plantation labor. Although the Portuguese and Japanese frequently migrated as entire families, most of the laborers who were imported to work in the fields were young men who oftentimes married within the local community of women (Nimmons 2011: 47).

CONCLUSION

America was and continues to be a land of opportunity for many native, indigenous populations as well as immigrants. Whether due to political persecution, indentured servitude, forced slavery, familial customs, or individual decision, all types of racial and ethnic populations came to North America to establish their own new cultural history. Their adaptation to the new world and new living situations brought various communities together, resulting in wide array of interracial relationships and marriages.

Regardless of the laws and endogamous rules (encouraging individuals of certain racial and ethnic backgrounds to marry within their race or ethnic group) that most populations adhered to, interracial relationships and marriages occurred and eventually increased. As each decade and century passed, more and more interracial relationships and marriages occurred. Their offspring, in turn, were categorized as what we now refer to as *multiracial populations*. This self-identification as "multiracial" is still a new racial concept that many are getting used to and embracing.

FIVE

The One-Drop Rule

INTRODUCTION

Let me go on record at the start of this discussion, admitting that I am truly embarrassed as an African American that the "one-drop rule" still exists in American culture in 2012. I am embarrassed as an American citizen that this concept serves multiple functions to differentiate one group of people from another. I am also embarrassed as an American citizen that the one-drop rule continues to be supported institutionally by a majority of the mainstream and African American organizations in the United States. Finally, I am embarrassed as an African American that a vast majority of African Americans stringently adhere culturally to the concept, as though it is badge of honor to designate anyone who has "one drop of black blood" as black, or African American, regardless of that person's other racial heritage or opinion.

I used to believe that I was in the "minority" among African Americans as thinking this way, yet I have been pleasantly surprised to find that there are others who feel the same as I do. For example, in 2011, I attended a Dr. Henry Louis Gates, Jr., lecture entitled "African-American Lives: Genetics, Genealogy, and Black History," held at East Carolina University. Dr. Gates is the Alphonse Fletcher University Professor and director of the W. E. B. DuBois Institute for African and African-American Research at Harvard University. He is also the author of several works of literary criticism, including *Figures in Black: Words, Signs, and the "Racial" Self* (Oxford University Press, 1989) and *The Signifying Monkey: A Theory of Afro-American Literary Criticism* (Oxford, 1989); the latter won the 1989

American Book award. During his lecture, Dr. Gates stated that he became obsessed with learning about his family's genealogy as early as the age of nine.

Dr. Gates also mentioned that although he may look black, he knows that his heritage also includes European and Native American. In fact, when Dr. Gates had a complete genetic profile completed, he discovered that he was 56% European (Irish), 37% African American, and 7% Native American. As a consequence, he considers himself more Irish than African American, thereby denouncing the one-drop rule that a vast majority of African Americans follow. Interestingly, at the conclusion of his lecture when asked by an audience member about the one-drop rule, Dr. Gates simply said, "Everybody's all mixed up."

So why is the one-drop rule still an issue today? In American culture, it means that a single drop of "black blood" makes a person a black. This concept is also known as the "one black ancestor rule" (Davis 1991; Sweet 2005; Zack 1993). Put simply, according to this idea, no matter what the race of the other parent is, if one of the parents is black, then the child will be considered black.

In the field of anthropology, the one-drop rule is referred to as "hypodescent" (Harris 1964; Kottack 2011) because it allocates children of a union between members of different groups to the minority group (*hypo* means "lower"). Hypodescent divides people into groups that have been unequal in their access to power, wealth, and prestige. Therefore, this American societal rule places blacks and all those who have any black ancestor, no matter how remote, in a lower class. But the question still remains: why would many blacks adhere to a one-drop rule that automatically places them in a lower social status? Later in this chapter, I will present some of the possible factors driving its continual use.

To get another initial perspective on the one-drop rule, consider the views of one of my key multiracial informants. When asked why it has taken the United States so long to recognize multiracial groups, my informant responded as follows:

I think there are several reasons. First of all, there are many more multiracial people who exist now than before. Secondly, even though many people of mixed heritage don't feel that they truly belong in one category or the other, those people were afraid to challenge the racist system of labeling people according to what was considered the least desirable race. I feel that today we still have a long way to go because many Americans of European descent don't want people with African ancestry polluting their race. I don't think they have a problem with multiracial people being acknowledged as multiracial, as long as we don't consider ourselves white, but many people of African descent want to include us in theirs. It seems to me that most black people feel the same about race as white people do—that black is undesirable and white is desirable. Therefore many black people want to point to multiracial people and say "look [how] white black people can look," which they can't do without us. I don't know why else black people want to hold on to the one-drop rule. I don't know why else they don't speak out against the racism of it. If black people were truly proud of being black, they wouldn't want us included in their race, especially those of us who are almost pure white. It seems that black people are trying to dilute their race and white people are trying to hold on to theirs.

This chapter examines the one-drop rule as it relates to American culture, and particularly how it has dramatically influenced race relations between blacks and whites in the United States. At one time, there may have been some justifiable reasons for its introduction and implementation in American society, but today it is truly antiquated. The one-drop rule has been and continues to be detrimental to all races, especially African Americans. The one group whose members truly recognize its devastating impact on American culture are multiracials, and we will show its negative cultural impact upon multiracials.

CULTURAL HISTORY OF THE ONE-DROP RULE

To grasp the significance of the one-drop rule and why it persists today, we have to examine its origins and the major factors for its use at various times in American history. Although this topic is highly controversial and many scholars, educators, and politicians do not want to admit its place in American and African American history, the facts remain that this rule dramatically affected blacks', whites', mulattoes', and multiracials' socioeconomic and political statuses. Therefore, a brief cultural historical review of the one-drop rule will help us to see its true function in our society.

Although many articles and books have been published about the one-drop rule, four major authors have provided an in-depth cultural evaluation of its function:

- Frank W. Sweet: *The Legal History of the Color Line* (2005)
- F. James Davis: *Who Is Black?* (1991)

- Naomi Zack: *Race and Mixed Race* (1993) and *American Mixed Race: The Culture of Microdiversity* (1995)
- Joel Williamson: *New People: Miscegenation and Mulattoes in the United States* (1980)

These authors' investigations and discussions of the major issues connected to the one-drop rule support my contention that this racial ruling should not have had a place in society in the past and, moreover, that it has no place in our society today.

Unlike other countries around the world, the United States is unique in its categorization of the black population. The U.S. Bureau of Census does not use a scientific definition when counting blacks (who were always counted as "Negroes" until 1980); instead, it uses the cultural definition of the one-drop rule. This one-drop rule of blackness became a formal law within American society and a cultural law within the black population.

In *Legal History of the Color Line: The Rise and Triumph of the One-Drop Rule*, Sweet (2005) examined the origin of the concept of the one-drop rule by reviewing travelers' accounts, diaries, fiction literature, advertisements for runaway slaves, and a database of 300 court cases adjudicated from 1770 to 1990 to resolve on which side of the color line an individual belonged. He found that the one-drop rule eventually became a national rule after a series of court decisions that punished whites and black for not honoring society's taboo against interracial dating and marriage.

Although there were a number of under-publicized historical facts related to the one-drop rule, Sweet (2005) contends one of most significant fact is that "the one drop rule was embraced by nineteenth-century Black leaders as a means of recognizing ethnicity" (339). The adherence to and implementation of the one-drop rule, however, varied in the American South and North (Sweet 2005).

Which major events caused the implementation of the one-drop rule in the South as well as in northern regions of the United States? Some scholars contend that it was the rising use of violence by blacks against whites as well as black leaders holding secret meetings in a number of states (Davis 1995; Sweet 2005).

The net effect of these three developments, along with, in later years, the Civil War, Reconstruction, and the Jim Crow system of segregation, solidified the one-drop rule not just in the South but also in the North. By 1915, the one-drop rule had become universally backed by whites in both South and North (Davis 1995: 122).

Yet blacks also supported the one-drop rule during these early years. Black migration to northern cities was accelerated by World War I. In the 1920s, laws blocking immigration from southern and eastern Europe, Asia, and Africa opened up low-cost housing in the inner cities for large numbers of southern blacks and Hispanic migrants. Davis observes that "mulattoes in New York's Harlem and other cities led the Black Renaissance of the 1920s, celebrating a black identity and a black culture rooted both in African and American experiences. By 1925, the American black community, including most mulattoes, firmly supported the one-drop rule" (1995: 123).

Davis (1995), however, adds that the strong attachment to and reinforcement of the one-drop rule among African Americans since 1925 has had costly effects within the black community. It has created dilemmas and traumas over personal identity, ambiguities and strains in everyday life, divisive conflicts over color in black families and communities, collective hysteria about passing and about invisible blackness, heavy pressure on light mulattoes to prove their blackness, administrative and legal problems of racial classification, misperceptions of the racial identities of huge populations in Asia and the Middle East, and failure to take miscegenation into proper account in scientific studies of African Americans (125).

In *Race and Mixed Race*, Zack (1993) goes further in her criticism as to why blacks have accepted this one-drop rule. Specifically, she makes the following argument:

It is not clear on the face of it why a black person, in the absence of racial neutrality, would want to impose a black designation on a racially mixed person. The more racially white any designated black person appears to be, the more the black racial designation of that person enforces the social devaluation of the black race. For anyone to insist that an individual be designated black solely on the strength of the racial designation of that individual's forebears merely enforces the idea that blackness is so terrible that neither individual identity, nor biological reality, nor generations of hereditary distance can erase it. (Zack 2005: 75)

THE CULTURAL IMPACT OF THE ONE-DROP RULE ON MULTIRACIALS

Although much attention has focused on blacks' and whites' adaptation to the one-drop rule over the years, very little attention has addressed its impact on multiracials. Culturally, multiracials have had to dramatically adjust to this one-drop rule over the years due to society's standards regarding black and white relationships. On the one hand, they must deny any black heritage completely if they are to maintain their place in mainstream white society. On the other hand, they must prove to blacks that they are "black enough."

Historically, there have been countless examples of persons of mixed heritage—particularly of black and white parentage—who had to keep their black heritage hidden. There was variation from one part of the country to another regarding the acceptance or denial of one's black heritage, yet the cultural pattern that many multiracials learned through time was to deny their black heritage over several generations. The denial of one's black heritage has caused many multiracials to question the cultural rules of mainstream white society.

Contrastingly, there have been countless examples of persons of mixed heritage—again particularly of black and white parentage—who had to accept their black heritage due to society's knowledge of that heritage and their physical traits (i.e., skin color, lips, hair). The cultural pattern that many multiracials learned was to develop a stronger affiliation with blacks by supporting black causes and cultural institutions, thereby visibly showing that they were culturally accepted by the black community.

Whether in the past or the present, the one-drop rule has caused many multiracials to make individual decisions that they may not have wanted to make. Numerous multiracials have been forced to decide to be a part of one racial group or another, owing to this antiquated, discriminatory, and racist societal unwritten rule.

To further emphasize my perspective regarding the discriminatory impact of the one-drop rule, the qualitative comments from key informant #3 support my contention. When asked, "How do you think 'non-multiracial' people perceive the growth of the multiracial population in the United States," she responded as follows:

It depends on the person individually. Unfortunately some African Americans are against it because they feel we are trying to distance ourselves from being black which is not the case. Those of us that are multiracial with black ancestry still refer to ourselves as black, but [as] black and white, or black and Asian, or black and Latino, et cetera. Some Caucasians are a bit more accepting but at times still try to place us in a one race category. I think we need more education as to why we identify as multiracial and what it exactly means.

CONCLUSION

This chapter examined the one-drop rule as it relates to American culture, and particularly how it has dramatically influenced race relations between blacks and whites in the United States. As with almost any unwritten societal rule, there are perceived justifications for its implementation and adherence to it by those who placed the cultural rule within a society. Historically, the one-drop rule performed its function in the United States by primarily separating racial groups from each other. Although it was not thoroughly accepted by all groups, it nonetheless remains a cultural fixture in American culture.

One group has consistently denounced this one-drop cultural rule both in the past and in the present—multiracials. When asked why it has taken the United States so long to recognize multiracial groups, the qualitative comment from informant #5 reflects how many multiracials feel about this issue:

I honestly think it has been a power struggle from the start. In early U.S. history, the majority race felt the need to keep the minority race separate and beneath them in order to remain in power. I think it has been an evolving struggle of letting go of that "power" and coming to acceptance.

PART III

Significant Biological, Health, and Lifestyle Issues

SIX

The Physical Features of Multiracial Populations

INTRODUCTION

A key issue that continues to be overlooked among multiracial populations is their physical features. The fact that multiracials are the offspring of two or more racially identified populations should warrant increased interest from biologists, physical anthropologists, geneticists, and other specialists who study the physical attributes of human populations, particularly when their numbers are drastically increasing every year. Yet for some unknown reason, this is not the case.

It is usually the general public who most often pays attention to and is always concerned about the physical features of multiracial individuals. For example, in an excellent article written by Indian American writer Nandini D'Souza entitled "Mistaken for the Nanny" (2010), the author had to come to terms with how the general public negatively reacted to the fact that she was the mother of a white, faired-skinned daughter. As she described herself and her husband at the beginning of the article:

I'm Indian, a medium to dark brown depending on the season. My husband, Myles, is Irish-German via Queens. He's milk white with blond hair and clear light-blue eyes. (123)

Before the couple's daughter, Asha, was born, D'Souza (2010) believed that she would look more Indian than anything else. To their surprise, Asha looked the exact opposite of her mother's preconceived ideals. Unfortunately, as Asha grew up, D'Souza and her husband experienced a wide variety of discriminatory reactions. At first, she tried to take the criticism in stride, believing that the comments were not mean; over time, however, they became unavoidable. There were a number of examples over the years that surprised them regarding the reaction of the general public to her daughter Asha.

Ultimately, D'Souza (2010) emphasized that she does not care what her daughter's physical features are. During some periods of the year, her daughter appears to favor her Indian side because of the increased sun exposure; overall, however, she favors her father's Irish German side.

D'Souza (2010) concludes her article with the following statement:

> She's too young to understand it, but I tell her often that she is going to change the world for the better, that children of mixed heritage will be the ones to someday figure out how to unite everyone. (123)

The physical attribute of "skin color" is still a significant issue in our society for all groups. It is a particularly sensitive topic for multiracial individuals and families, who bring to the fore a unique cultural societal issue in a manner unlike any other racial population in the United States.

Why is it that our society feels so uncomfortable with people who are either "light skinned" or "dark skinned" and whose family members may be of a different color? It is not as if this issue has not occurred with other ethnic and racial populations in the past (African Americans, Hispanic/ Latinos, Asians, Native Americans), yet with individuals who are classified as multiracial and those who prefer to be classified as multiracial, it can become a major problem in a person's life or in his or her family relations. Thus skin color, along with all the other physical attributes (i.e., hair, nose, eyes, lips and body build) associated with multiracials, becomes another aspect of a racial issue that our society has not truly understood and accepted.

DEFINING RACE

The issue of race remains a highly controversial topic for most people to discuss and research. In Western society, the term "race" is more often used for social and political purposes, rather than in its biological meaning. When the term "race" is more associated with its biological meaning, it does convey certain mixed messages that may be viewed as being biased toward (or against) some groups or individuals.

Anthropologists consider the meaning of race in two different ways. For example, physical anthropologists look at the biological characteristics of human populations in different areas of the world. They compare these populations to one another with the goal of understanding the patterning of human biological variation. In the 19th century, anthropologists studied the bodily characteristics of humans: their skin color, the color and texture of their hair, the proportions of their limbs, the features of their faces and bodies, and the internal details of flesh and bone that make us both physically unique and similar to other people. Some of this early physical categorization of human biological variation, however, was blatantly used to stereotype various human populations. In the 20th century, studies of more subtle variation—of blood groups and antibody types and, most recently, of genetic material—have added new levels of detail and complexity to that research.

The other major approach to race is to focus on human cultures and behavior. Cultural anthropologists study the ways in which people are highly influenced by their social and cultural environment. From this perspective, "race" is conceived of as a cultural construction, not a biological fact. This ideology of race may use the language of physical features when discussing group differences, but biology and the biological characteristics of humans are not of fundamental importance in how these groups are defined. The question before anthropologists in this case is, How and why do people use cultural criteria to define human races, and how have these definitions changed over time?

Here are some typical definitions of the word "race":

Race is defined as persons who are relatively homogeneous with respect to biological inheritance. (Scupin 2003)

Race is defined as a scientific, biogenetic concept, a phenotypically and/or geographically distinctive subspecific group, composed of individuals inhabiting a defined geographic and/or ecological region, and possessing characteristic phenotypic and gene frequencies that distinguish it from such groups. (Scupin 2003)

Human races are generally defined in terms of original geographic range and common hereditary traits which may be morphological, serological, hematological, immunological, or biochemical. (Scupin 2003)

As you can see, there is a great deal of variation in the definition of race in Western society. For the sake of the discussion here, we associate the term more with its social and cultural constructs, rather its biological constructs. If we take this perspective, we can better understand certain ethnic groups' (i.e., multiracials, African Americans, Latino Americans, European Americans, Asian Americans, and American Indians) preferences for certain types of physical features.

ENCULTURATION OF PREFERRED PHYSICAL FEATURES

In this book, we define culture as a system of shared beliefs, values, and traditions that are transmitted from generation to generation through learning. Culture plays a vital role in shaping all of our beliefs, attitudes, and behaviors—including our preferences for certain physical features (i.e., skin color, height, weight, hair texture, eye color, body type, and body image). For example, in the United States, the social and cultural preoccupation with skin color has always been and continues to be a major factor in determining an individual's social status both within one's familial network and in mainstream society. But how do individuals within a society learn which values, beliefs, and patterns are preferred among the members of their society? This process is referred to as enculturation.

Enculturation is defined as the process whereby individuals learn the behavioral standards of a particular cultural trait within their society or group. Enculturation is a process, because usually individuals go through a series of steps (success and failures) that determine whether they meet with approval or acceptance based on that cultural trait in a particular group (i.e., ethnic, social, educational, gender, or age groups).

One of the best ways to see how enculturation really works is to examine its attributes. The major attributes of enculturation are sixfold:

1. It is a learned process.
2. It is transmitted by symbols.
3. It adds meaning to reality.
4. It is differently shared.
5. It is integrated.
6. It is adaptive.

Enculturation relates directly to our preferred physical features, because all of us learn preferred physical features for women, men, boys, and girls that are highly influenced by immediate family members, extended family members, friends, social groups, and ethnic groups, as well as mainstream society's groupings. For example, in *Black America, Body Beautiful*, Bailey (2008) found that African Americans had varying preferences of beauty and body images for men and women.

Enculturation is transmitted by symbols, both verbal and nonverbal. In the diet and fitness field, U.S. society tends to show a preference for certain body types (thin to slim) in magazines, television programs, advertisements, and the entertainment world that are perceived as healthy; in contrast, those persons who do not fit this category (those who are full figured or shapely) are not perceived as healthy. Symbolically, the approved body types (thin to slim) become the norm in society and do not allow for much variation.

Enculturation adds meaning to reality. For example, children, adolescents, and adults participate in beauty contests to find out whether they are the most "beautiful" in their age category. If a certain individual, with a certain body type, is selected as the winner of a beauty contest, then it is not only her personality but also her body type being selected as representing society's standards for beauty.

Enculturation is differently shared. In general, African Americans view body image differently than European Americans, for instance. Not only is there variation between African Americans and European Americans, but there is also much variation in beliefs about body image within the African American population.

Enculturation is integrated. In other words, an individual's preferred physical features must be viewed as integrated into the totality of one's life, because they may be directly related to the individual's income (whether the person can afford to modify his or her physical features through surgery or exercise), geographic location (whether he or she lives in an area that promotes certain physical features—for instance, thinner body types on the West Coast, heavier body types in the Southeast), and historical issues (whether the person has had a history, either family or individual, of acknowledging the importance of certain physical features, such as lighter skin color).

Finally, enculturation is adaptive. For more members of the general public to accept certain physical features, the public needs to have more opportunities to see the type of physical features highly valued in a society. If this adaptive strategy were incorporated on a regular basis, then we would be better able to see and appreciate not only how multiracials' physical features are changing how we view them, but also how multiracials' preferred physical features are changing U.S. society.

To date—perhaps not surprisingly—there has been little research on the enculturation of preferred physical features among racial and ethnic groups in America. To better illustrate how some ethnic groups in the United States have enculturated certain types of preferences for physical features, this chapter presents a review of the latest studies and data. This brief review for each ethnic group is intended to help us understand the impact of mainstream societal standards of preferred physical features upon the various racial and ethnic groups' preferences for certain type of physical features. Not surprisingly, these preferred physical features among various racial and ethnic groups in America also influence the preferred physical features among multiracials.

We must first define the major racial and ethnic groups in the United States. This chapter uses the categories of ethnicity in the United States defined in Directive 15 of the U.S. Office of Management and Budget (OMB), which established standards for the collection of data on race and ethnicity. The original version of OMB Directive 15 was released in 1977; the second version was issued in 1997. The goal of the directive is as follows:

> [T]o provide consistent and comparable data on race and ethnicity throughout the federal government for an array of statistical and administrative programs. Development of the data standards stems in large measure from new responsibilities to enforce civil rights laws. Data were needed to monitor equal access to housing, education, and employment opportunities for population groups that historically had experienced discrimination and different treatment because of their race or ethnicity.

Here are the categories of race according to the second version of OMB Directive 15 (Office of Management and Budget 1977):

1. American Indian or Alaska Native—a person having origins in any of the original peoples of North America, and who maintains cultural identification, tribal affiliation, or community recognition.

2. Asian—a person having origins in any of the original peoples of the Far East, Southeast Asia, or the Indian subcontinent, including, for example, Cambodia, China, India, Japan, Korea, Malaysia, Pakistan, the Philippine Islands, Thailand, and Vietnam.

3. Native Hawaiian or other Pacific Islander—a person having origins in any of the original peoples of Hawaii, Guam, Samoa, or the other Pacific Islands.

4. Black—a person having origins in any of the black racial groups of Africa.

5. Hispanic/Latino—a person having origins in any of the original peoples of Mexico, Puerto Rico, Cuba, Central and South America, and other Spanish-speaking countries.

6. White—a person having origins in any of the original peoples of Europe, North Africa, or the Middle East.

ENCULTURATION OF EUROPEAN AMERICANS' PREFERRED PHYSICAL FEATURES

Research indicates that preferred body images vary among cultures, as well as within cultures across groups and time. Within Western industrialized cultures, there have been many changes over the years in the body shape and size that are considered attractive and healthy, especially for women.

Preferred Female Physical Features

Historically in Western industrialized cultures, plumpness was considered fashionable and erotic. From the Middle Ages, artists idealized the "reproductive figure." The fullness of the stomach was emphasized as a symbol of fertility. The female body was frequently represented with full, rounded hips and breasts. This trend is represented in popular paintings of the 1600s, which portrayed a woman with a plump body—the preferred body type of the time (Bailey 2008).

The idealization of slimness in women is a very recent phenomenon, dating from the 1920s. Many scholars contend that the thin ideal is the result of successful marketing by the fashion industry, which has become the standard of cultural beauty in the affluent industrialized societies of the 20th century. Fashions in clothing were represented by hand-drawn illustrations until the 1920s, when they started to be photographed and widely distributed in mass-market fashion magazines. These magazines presented a fantasy image of how women should look. The fashions themselves demanded a molding of the female body because each "look" suited a particular body shape (Bailey 2008).

In the 1930s and 1940s, ideals of beauty moved toward a shapelier figure. For instance, the mean measurements of Miss America pageant winners went from 30-25-32 (inches) in the early 1920s to 35-25-36 (inches) in the 1940s. Famous actresses such as Lana Turner and Jane Russell typified the change of preferred body images and types during this period.

Although this trend toward appreciation of fuller-figure women in American continued in the 1950s (e.g., with the emergence of Marilyn Monroe), there was also a significant move toward slimness. Actresses such as Grace Kelly and Audrey Hepburn became role models for some young women, and the idealization of slimness became particularly acute in the 1960s, when the fashion model Twiggy became the role model for a generation of young women. Twiggy's body type was described as a "flat-chested, boyish figure, and [she] weighed 96 lbs" (Bailey 2008: 15).

Slimness or a thin-looking body type came to symbolize unconventionality, freedom, youthfulness, and the "jet set" lifestyle. This trend spread across Europe and the United States and became the foundation of the fashion industry and major media's preferences in female body types. Therefore, thin and thinner became the standard of beauty for many women from the 1960s to today. In fact, in 2008 in the fashion industry, extreme thinness was the preferred body type for female models (Bailey 2008).

Explanations for this preference for thin physical features include a desire to emulate the upper class and the fashion industry, where thinness is equated with wealth, leisure, and fame; women's roles changing from maternal to more instrumental or masculine venues and occupations; a desire to appear youthful; and a perceived association between thinness and health, as promoted by the medical community. The potentially negative consequences of the thin ideal include negative body image, low self-esteem, and psychological and physical disorders of life-threatening proportions (Bailey 2008).

Preferred Male Physical Features

Western representations of the male body also have an interesting history. Contemporary Western cultures derive much of their preferences in male physical features from ancient Greece and Rome. Sculptors in ancient Greece were keenly interested in the problems of realistically representing the human figure, and it was during this time in history that life-like male nudes started to become more visible. Men were often depicted as nude, whereas women were depicted clothed in cloaks and undergarments. The male body was admired and considered more attractive than the female body (Bailey 2008).

In the seventh century BC, there emerged a trend favoring a broad-shouldered, narrow-hipped ideal that has become known as the Daedalic style, after the mythical Daedalus of Crete, who was, according to legend, the first Greek sculptor. At this stage, the male body was admired and presented in a strictly stylized manner, with emphasis on clearly defined muscles that were carved into the surface of marble sculptures (Bailey 2008).

Contemporary Western cultures also admired classic Roman male figures that were illustrated as slender and muscular in paintings and sculptures. The male body continued to dominate art until the mid-1800s (Bailey 2008).

By the end of the 19th century, the impact of sports culture had transformed the Western perspective on male bodies. The celebration of youthfulness and exuberance directed the analytical schema of advertisers that equated physical activity, especially those activities associated with sports, and its effects on the male body as the ideal to strive for.

In 1921, when Charles Atlas (born Angelo Siciliano) won the "World's Most Beautiful Man Contest," his victory helped solidify the connection between the body and physical fitness. In the following year, Atlas was declared "America's Most Perfectly Developed Man." The Charles Atlas body was described as muscular, smooth, and well proportioned, evoking perfect manhood and confidence. It is interesting that what Charles Atlas sold was less about his body and more about the image of confidence in one's physical self—an ebullient "body love" in which the body seemed less important than the freedom to love it.

Today, the preferred male body type is slender and moderately muscular. According to Bailey (2008), the sociocultural pressure on men is different and less extreme than that on women, as men are still judged in terms of their achievements rather than their looks. Yet this trend has drastically changed in the past few years. European American men are under increased sociocultural pressure to conform to the muscular, well-toned mesomorphic (medium-sized) shape, and most scholars expect this cultural shift to continue for decades (Bailey 2008).

ENCULTURATION OF HISPANIC/LATINOS' PREFERRED PHYSICAL FEATURES

Although numerous studies have investigated mainstream European American cultures' preferences for certain body types and images, very few historical and contemporary studies have focused on the preferences of other ethnic populations, such as the Hispanics/Latinos. According to the U.S. Census Bureau, in 1980 there were approximately 14.6 million Hispanics/Latinos living in the United States. By 2000, that number had dramatically increased by nearly 142 percent, to 35.3 million. Currently, the Hispanic/Latino population is the largest ethnic minority group in the United States.

The umbrella term "Hispanic" is used to conveniently describe a large and diverse population. A person with a Hispanic/Latino background is someone for whom the conditions and events surrounding and influencing his or her life, including education, language, experiences, and health beliefs, are associated with Spanish civilization. Each Hispanic group, however, is distinct and unique, with its own history. Each group has its own relation to this country, and each tends to be concentrated in different geographical areas.

The Hispanic/Latino population in the United States is divided into five main subgroups: Mexican Americans, Puerto Ricans, Cuban Americans, Central and South Americans, and people of other Hispanic origins. Mexican Americans are the largest subgroup, representing nearly 60 percent of the Hispanic/Latino population, and Puerto Ricans are the second largest. Together, they account for more than two-thirds of the Hispanic/Latino population.

Interestingly, the majority of the body image studies regarding the Hispanic/Latino population have been comparative studies conducted alongside European Americans. Although evidence from these studies suggests that the preferred body images for Hispanics/Latinos do not differ from those for European Americans, one study contradicted this finding.

Altabe (1998) found that Hispanic/Latino adults had a more positive body image, as indicated by higher self-ratings of attractiveness in comparison to European Americans. In that qualitative analysis of ideal traits, both Hispanic/Latino and European American college students (men and women) valued being tall and tan. The European Americans idealized blond hair, whereas Hispanic/Latinos idealized brown hair and brown eyes. Thus the typical Hispanic/Latino physical features (brown hair and eyes, darker skin) were viewed positively by this sample.

Overall, issues of general appearance and ideal Hispanic/Latino physical features have not been investigated in any great depth. Because the majority of the studies on Hispanic/Latino culture have been comparative studies, more culture-specific studies need to be conducted to discover the diversity of ideals regarding body images. The ideal of thinness in Hispanic/Latino culture is relatively new and may not be the representative preference of the entire group. Therefore, the diversity of the Hispanic/Latino population, which includes Cubans, Puerto Ricans, Mexicans, Central Americans, South Americans, and persons of other Spanish cultural origins, need to be researched.

ENCULTURATION OF ASIANS' AND PACIFIC ISLANDERS' PREFERRED PHYSICAL FEATURES

Another population that has received very little attention regarding their opinions and beliefs on preferred physical features are Asians and Pacific Islanders. Asian Americans are defined as the federally designated ethnic populations whose origins are in Asia. Individuals of Asian descent who are U.S. citizens or permanent residents of the country are considered Asian Americans. According to U.S. Census designations, Asian Americans include, but are not limited to, those persons who self-classify as Asian Indians, Cambodians, Chinese, Filipino, Hmong, Japanese, Korean, Laotian, Thai, Vietnamese, and "other."

Pacific Islanders are defined as individuals who are descendants of the original residents of the Pacific Islands under the jurisdiction of the U.S. government. According to the U.S. Census designation, Pacific Islanders include, but are not limited to, Chamorro, Hawaiians, Melanesians, Micronesians, Polynesians, Samoans, and "other" Pacific Islanders.

More than 30 different ethnic subgroups make up the Asian and Pacific Islander populations, with each subgroup having its distinctive cultural traditions, languages, and values. There is a great deal of intra-group and inter-group variability among members of the Asian and Pacific Islander population in terms of the degree of acculturation, generation, and immigration experiences. Despite this variability, similarities in terms of traditional cultural values, status as an ethnic minority group, and particular physical features (which may differ from Western notions of beauty) also exist.

For example, recent studies among Pacific Islanders (adults identified as Native Hawaiians, Samoans, Tongans, Cook Islanders, and Maori) showed that they preferred a larger body size than European Americans. In addition, one study showed that Pacific Islanders with a higher body mass index (BMI) were more likely to see themselves as "underweight" or the "right weight" in comparison to European Americans. These findings are consistent with traditional views among Pacific Islanders that place great importance on larger body size, as it represents high status, power, authority, and wealth.

Some Asian cultures, such as those in Korea, China, Japan, and the other Philippines, have traditionally viewed obesity as a sign of prosperity, good health, or beauty. Current research and observations indicate that this is no longer the case among young women in modern industrialized Asia.

Comparative studies of Asians and Pacific Islanders with European Americans have provided inconsistent findings. For example, an analysis of 22 studies on body image or other related behaviors in Asians and European Americans produced three sets of findings:

1. Asians showed more concerns than European Americans about their body image.

2. Asians showed no differences with European Americans about their body image.

3. Asian males had fewer concerns than European American males about their body image.

One major factor that may mediate and/or moderate body image concerns and change strategies among Asian cultural groups is that, unlike in Western culture, some cultures, such as the Chinese, do not place as much importance on male muscularity.

Recently, an academic team conducted a two-study research program on male body images in Taiwan and Western society. The team hypothesized that Taiwanese men would exhibit less dissatisfaction with their bodies than their Western counterparts, and that Taiwanese advertising would place less value on the male body than Western media.

For the first study, 55 Taiwanese male undergraduate students at a university in Taiwan were recruited. The self-identified heterosexual male students participated in this study "examining body image perception," in which their height, weight, and body fat were measured, followed by their completion of a brief computerized test. The results from this phase of the study were then compared with previous results of testing of men from the United States and Europe. The researchers found that men in both the East and the West preferred to be more muscular. When the study participants were asked to identify which male body type women preferred, however, the Taiwanese man appeared much more comfortable with their body image than their Western counterparts. Further investigation found that American men estimated only a 5 pound difference between actual weight and ideal body image.

For the second study, the research team compared the value of the male body in American versus Taiwanese magazine advertising, using a method of counting dressed and undressed models in women's magazines. They chose two leading women's magazines from the United States, *Cosmopolitan* and *Glamour*. For Taiwan, they chose the comparable *Bella* and *Vivi*, as well as the Taiwanese version of *Cosmopolitan* (Yang, Gray, and Pope 2002).

In the Taiwanese magazines, Yang et al. (2002) found more than 1,000 advertisements that used male or female models, advertising a wide variety of products—some body-related (e.g., clothes, perfume) and others not (e.g., tobacco)—from Asian and Western manufacturers. When they compared the Taiwanese advertisements (from 2001) with their earlier American data, the researchers found only gradual differences in the prevalence of undressed models of both sexes, even though the Taiwanese magazines actually showed more nudity. Asian women, however, were portrayed undressed only about half as often as Western women in the Taiwanese magazines, and Asian men were almost never shown undressed. Of the 78 Asian men in the Taiwanese magazine advertisements, only 4 (5%) were shown undressed, compared to 43 percent of Western women in the same magazines.

The researchers concluded from their two studies ("Body Image in Taiwanese Men and Male Body Image in Taiwanese and American Magazine Advertising") that Western culture has become much more focused on male body appearance than Chinese culture (98% of the Taiwanese population is of Chinese origin—hence the use of the term "Chinese culture") (Yang et al. 2002). The researchers contend that this difference primarily reflects how Chinese culture places less emphasis on muscularity as a means of demonstrating masculinity.

Overall, the differences in preferred physical features among Asians and Pacific Islanders have been found to be the result of either an increase in or lack of exposure to Western cultures. Although younger Asian and Asian American women are probably aware of traditional Asian ideals that promote weight gain, they seem to be more likely to subscribe to Western ideals of thinness. Moreover, as in Western cultures, there appears to be less of an emphasis on physical appearance for men, so less is known about the ideal body image of Asian and Asian American men. Additional research, particularly qualitative research that asks Asian American and Pacific Islander women and men what they perceive to be the traditional ideals of beauty, would elucidate the difference between traditional and Western notions of beauty (Bailey 2008).

ENCULTURATION OF NATIVE AMERICANS' AND ALASKA NATIVES' PREFERRED PHYSICAL FEATURES

Another population that has received very little attention and research regarding their opinions and beliefs about preferred physical features are the Native American and Alaska Native populations. In the few studies conducted on body image in these populations, Native Americans displayed more concern with their body image than did European Americans (Bailey 2008).

One of the major factors that may affect the differences observed between Native Americans and European Americans is BMI. Where assessed, Native Americans had a higher BMI, and they were more likely to perceive themselves as overweight in comparison to European Americans. However, the higher levels of concern with body image and symptoms of eating disorders found among First Nations may also be indicative of the feelings of displacement and alienation in urban areas, a loss of their ethnic identity, and a nonsupportive community. As with other ethnic minorities, an important factor to further examine is the individual identification with his or her own cultural group (Bailey 2008).

ENCULTURATION OF AFRICAN AMERICANS' PREFERRED PHYSICAL FEATURES

To provide an understanding of African Americans' preferred physical features, this section highlights two innovative studies that capture their perspectives.

First, a study conducted by Altabe (1998) surveyed 150 male and 185 female college students attending the University of South Florida. Participants completed four different body image questionnaires and several self-ratings that included physical attractiveness and physical appearance and were scored on a scale of 1 to 11. Qualitative results from the sampled African Americans, Asian Americans, Caucasian Americans, and Hispanic/Latino Americans revealed specific preferences for each group as well as for men and women. Greater height was preferred by all racial/ethnic groups. With regard to hair and skin color preferences, however, there were distinctive differences, such as non-Caucasian females wanted longer hair and all groups valued dark skin or wanted darker skin, except for African American females and Asian males.

Another study on the body image of college-age subjects, titled "Comparison of Body Image Dimensions by Race/Ethnicity and Gender in a University Population," had three major objectives: (1) to examine the interaction of gender and race or ethnicity on body image dimensions, including three racial or ethnic groups in the sample; (2) to more comprehensively measure body image by assessing feelings about body parts significant to race or ethnicity; and (3) to measure and control for numerous important possible factors including age, body size, socioeconomic status, and social desirability (Miller et al. 2000). In general, there were distinct preferences among the various racial and ethnic groups of college students, and culture impacted their decisions.

THE IMPACT OF MULTIRACIAL PHYSICAL FEATURES IN AMERICA

One of the most interesting aspects of multiracial physical features is their impact on the standard of beauty in America. Beauty experts in the

United States have noted that as the ethnic demographics of the population change, so do the ideals of beauty in women. According to Blended People of America (2010), the increased popularity of multiracial celebrity women adds to the current appeal of the ethnic look and preferred physical features associated with women such as fuller lips, fuller figures, and even wider noses. Physical features that were once deemed unattractive are now being embraced by ethnic women themselves and some of their Caucasian peers. This is a clear sign of the times: with many developed nations turning into cultural melting pots, it is only natural for ideals and perceptions of beauty to shift toward matching the new face of society.

In fact, a research study in the United Kingdom recently found that people of mixed race were considered the most attractive and successful as opposed to other groups. In this research conducted at Cardiff University's School of Psychology, the research team collected a random sample of 1,205 black, white, and mixed-race faces from Facebook communities (Lewis 2010). Each face was then rated for its perceived attractiveness relative to others on a scale of one to 10 by 40 female students. Overall, there was a 55 percent chance of mixed-race faces being perceived as more attractive than either black or white faces. Researchers contend that this British study is another indication that multiracial physical features have rapidly become the most preferred physical features from one country to another.

CONCLUSION

Interestingly, the one attribute that is often overlooked when we speak about multiracials is their physical features. Although those persons who are not multiracial will constantly inquire about and ask questions as to which group a multiracial may belong to, serious open discussion about these persons' physical features is usually squelched because many people do not want to appear to be insensitive.

In today's society, the physical features of multiracials are often held in high esteem and are considered desirable physical attributes by many around the world. The cosmetic and beauty industries are profiting from the wide variety of products and devices used for making one's skin either slightly tan or lighter for women, relaxing one's hair, or injecting collagen in one's lips to make them fuller—all of which are direct outcomes of how the physical features often associated with various ethnic and racial groups, including multiracials, have become highly valued.

SEVEN

Multiracial Health Disparities

INTRODUCTION

One of the most difficult aspects of providing definitive statements or conclusions about specific populations in the United States is that there must be some type of reliable data or database that represents them. The U.S. Census is one such reliable source for specific databases. Since 1790, the United States has depended on its 10-year census to collect population data across the country. Despite all of its flaws in undercounting and overcounting various populations over the centuries, the federal government's U.S. Census reporting is the best federal system for tabulating population data.

Although we have finally started to collect pools of data on multiracial populations across the country, we have not yet collected data on their particular health and medical issues. Such data simply are not being collected in specific detail by various county, state, and federal agencies as of 2013. As a consequence, we must rely upon the few scholars and research studies focused on various multiracial health and medical issues to provide us with some small insight into multiracials' particular health and medical issues.

The primary intent of this chapter is not only to present the latest health disparities data on specific racial and ethnic populations in the United States, but also to highlight how multiracial and multiethnic populations think and feel about specific health and medical issues affecting their family members and friends. Very few studies have attempted to understand the perspectives of multiracials on various health and medical issues, primarily because the vast majority of scholars and researchers have not considered it a topic worthy of investigation. Fortunately, times are rapidly changing and many multiracial and multiethnic persons are expressing their concerns and perspectives on a number of significant health and medical issues. This chapter focuses on the following aspects of this discussion: (1) current racial and ethnic health disparity data; (2) multiracials' identity and its relationship to health care interactions; (3) multiracials' views on race-based therapeutics; and (4) multiracials' health disparities and the connections between race, ancestry, and genetics.

CURRENT RACIAL AND ETHNIC HEALTH DISPARITY DATA

According to the Office of Minority Health and Health Disparities at the Centers for Disease Control and Prevention (www.cdc.gov/omhd), it is very difficult today to make generalizations about which health conditions are most prevalent among multiracial Americans, as little research to date has focused on this group. Even the Department of Health and Health Services in its latest plan to reduce racial and ethnic health disparities, entitled *A Nation Free of Disparities in Health and Health Care* (http://minorityhealth.hhs.gov), does not mention the word "multiracial" or any plans related to reducing health disparities among multiracial Americans. In the coming years as more health data are collected, however, a clearer picture of the health status of multiracial Americans will likely emerge (McNeil 2011).

In the meantime, we must rely on the traditional racial and ethnic health disparity data and data sets to provide us with general guides as to the types of health and medical issues related to multiracial populations in the United States (Bailey 2000, 2006). Regardless of how limiting these data are, and how stereotypical they are regarding each very broad-based racial and ethnic population, the data do give health practitioners, public health professionals, and health policy administrators a direction for planning future initiatives and programs for multiracial populations across the country, simply because what is happening to the current single-group racial and ethnic populations will likely relate in some way to various multiracial populations.

Infant Mortality

One of the health indicators most often used to determine the health status of a population or a country is infant mortality (Centers for Disease

Control and Prevention 1999, 2011). MacDorman and Mathews (2011: 49) state that "the U.S. infant mortality rate (the number of deaths among infants aged <1 year per 1,000 births) declined from approximately 100 deaths per 1,000 births in 1900 to 6.89 in 2000." However, the rate did not decline substantially from 2000 to 2005. In addition, MacDorman and Mathews (2011) emphasize that for certain racial/ethnic groups, the infant mortality rates have not improved at all.

For example, in MacDorman and Mathews' (2012) report, "Infant Deaths—United States, 2000–2007," the authors note that among racial/ethnic minority groups, the highest infant mortality rate—that for non-Hispanic black women (13.35 infant deaths per 1,000 live births)—was 2.4 times higher than the rate for non-Hispanic white women (5.58/1,000). Additionally, the infant mortality rates for American Indian/Alaska Native women (8.28/1,000) and for Puerto Rican women (8.01/1,000) were higher than the rate for non-Hispanic white women (5.58/1,000). 8.28/1,000).

Traditionally, infant mortality has been a very challenging medical and public health issue to address. MacDorman and Mathews (2011: 50) emphasize that "the United States appears unlikely to meet its national health objective for 2010 of an infant mortality rate of 4.5 infant deaths per 1,000 live births or the overarching goals of eliminating disparities among racial/ethnic populations."

The recent plateau in the U.S. infant mortality rate and the long-standing racial/ethnic disparities continue to raise concern among researchers and policymakers. For example, the difference in the infant mortality rate for non-Hispanic whites and non-Hispanic blacks was 138.4 percent in 2000 and 139.2 percent in 2006 (MacDorman and Mathews 2011). Prevention of preterm births is critical to lower the overall infant mortality rate and reduce racial/ethnic disparities (MacDorman and Mathews 2011: 50).

We can only speculate about the infant mortality rate among multiracials. Based on the current data, there is reason for optimism that their rates might be as low or lower than the rates for Mexican Americans, Asian/Pacific Islanders, and Central and South Americans—but they might also be as high as or higher than the rates for non-Hispanic blacks. It is very important to speculate about and discuss this significant health issue of infant mortality among multiracials, primarily because we can plan more effectively now and in the next few years, when we will have enough sufficient and reliable data on multiracial health disparity issues to address them properly.

Obesity

How prevalent is obesity among Americans? According to the Centers for Disease Control and Prevention (CDC), for the first time in history, there are more overweight and obese people in the nation than people of normal weight. According to a report entitled "Prevalence of Overweight and Obesity Among Adults: United States, 1999," initial results from the 1999 National Health and Nutrition Examination Survey, using measured heights and weights, indicate that an estimated 61 percent of U.S. adults are either overweight or obese.

Among ethnic minority groups, the prevalence of obesity among blacks increased from 19 percent in 1991 to 27 percent in 1998. This is a 39 percent increase. Among Hispanics, the prevalence of obesity increased from 12 percent in 1991 to 21 percent in 1998—an 80 percent increase (Mokdad et al. 1999: 1520; Flegal 1998; Freeman 2011; Guyer et al. 2000).

As with all racial/ethnic populations, one can only speculate and estimate the obesity prevalence rate among multiracials. Multiracials may have the lowest obesity prevalence or the highest, or they may fall within the middle of all racial/ethnic groups. Although the percentage of multiracials who could be classified as obese is unknown, investigating their contributing biologic, social, and cultural factors may give new insight into the issues of obesity for all populations.

AIDS and HIV Infection

Acquired immunodeficiency syndrome (AIDS) is a disease in which the body's immune system breaks down. The immune system fights off infections and certain other diseases. Because the system fails, a person with AIDS develops a variety of life-threatening illnesses (CDC 1993, 2008).

The human immunodeficiency virus (HIV) causes AIDS. People infected with HIV can develop many health problems, including extreme weight loss, severe pneumonia, cancer, and damage to the nervous system. These illnesses signal the onset of AIDS. In some people, these illnesses may develop within a year or two after the initial infection. Other individuals may stay healthy for as long as 10 or more years before symptoms appear.

Approximately 1.1 million adults and adolescents are living with HIV infection in the United States, with 48,200 to 64,500 persons being newly infected each year (CDC 2006; Hall et al. 2008). According to the CDC (1982: 87), "at the beginning of the HIV epidemic in the United States in the early 1980s, the majority of persons with an HIV diagnosis were white men who have sex with men (MSM)."

African Americans constitute a substantially large percentage of AIDS cases nationally. In 1992, African Americans represented 29 percent of the reported AIDS cases. In 1993, the AIDS rate for African American females (73 per 100,000) was approximately 15 times greater than that for Caucasian females (5 per 100,000). The rate for African American males in 1993 was five times greater than that for Caucasian males.

Recently, a CDC study analyzed data from a national HIV surveillance system. In the 37 states for which data were analyzed, "a total of 35,526 persons aged > 13 years received a diagnosis of HIV in 2005, and 34,038 received such a diagnosis in 2008" (Hall et al. 2011: 87). Interesting, data were also collected from multiracials, and rates varied among specific groups.

Unlike with the previously mentioned health disparity data (infant mortality and obesity), U.S. government public health agencies have collected substantial data on HIV infections among persons of multiple races (multiracials). This is remarkable particularly at a time when most public health officials and administrators (federal and state) indicate that there are not enough data on multiracials to draw any firm conclusions regarding their health status. Presently, this CDC data show that multiracials' HIV infection rates are the lowest of all groups' rates and that HIV prevalence among multiracials continues to decrease. This finding should be further investigated in detail because it could obviously lead to a new set of cultural health disparity issues and program development that is effective not just for multiracials but for all HIV-infected groups in the United States.

MULTIRACIALS' IDENTITY AND ITS RELATIONSHIP TO HEALTH CARE INTERACTIONS

In one of the most innovative and early studies on multiracial people, Phillips, Odunlami, and Bonham (2007), from the National Human Genome Research Institute at the National Institutes of Health, investigated perceptions, beliefs, and values of individuals whose parents are from different racial backgrounds. The objective of the study was to gather new information about the participants' perceptions of their identity, their social and clinical experiences as multiracial individuals, and their opinions on the debate regarding the importance of human genetic variation in understanding health disparities and use of race-based therapies. This qualitative research study interviewed 22 individuals of African and European backgrounds in two metropolitan areas (Washington, D.C., and Atlanta, Georgia).

Consistent with other findings, Phillips et al. (2007: 813) found that "participants' identity was influenced by a number of personal, social and contextual factors." Physical appearance and racial labels often affected the individual's personal identity. In general, "participants seemed concerned about the social implications of creating race-based therapeutics and that using genetics provided an additional treatment option for different groups" (807).

So what can we take away from Phillips et al.'s (2007) qualitative study of multiracial individuals? In particular, this study suggests that "the perspectives of multiracial individuals charge researchers to address the challenges that we face within our current racial classification system and biomedical research" (Phillips et al. 2007: 815).

CONCLUSION

Although there have been very scant group data collected on multiracial health status and conditions to date, the time to do so is now. It is critical for all agencies—local, state, and federal—to establish reliable databases on health, medical, and cultural health issues associated with multiracial populations throughout the United States. The fact that their numbers will double and triple within the next decade demands every agency's attention and respect, as well as program development addressing a wide array of multiracial health disparity issues.

Multiracial health disparities is such a new health and medical issue that many agencies, researchers, health administrators, and politicians are hesitant to take the lead in supporting its rightful place among groups' other health disparity concerns. This issue has ramifications not only in health care but, more importantly, in the politics of health care. The individual and/or agency that will take the lead in addressing multiracial health disparities at a very significant level will be the one person and/or agency that will be considered a pioneer when we look back on this time period 50 years from now.

EIGHT

Multiracials and Bone Marrow Transplants

INTRODUCTION

The vast majority of the health and medical issues associated with multiracials in the United States are still relatively new to most Americans. Many are oblivious to the fact that multiracials suffer countless barriers in attempting to seek specialized medical care for a wide variety of illnesses and diseases from well-established medical facilities and health care systems. One of the major concerns involves their ability to obtain bone marrow transplants.

Bone marrow is the soft, fatty tissue inside an individual's bones. Stem cells are immature cells in the bone marrow that give rise to all of the blood cells. Blood is made of three components:

- Red blood cells (which carry oxygen to the body's tissues)
- White blood cells (which fight infection)
- Platelets (which help the blood clot)

A bone marrow transplant delivers healthy bone marrow stem cells into the patient. It replaces bone marrow that is either not working properly or has been destroyed by chemotherapy or radiation. Three kinds of bone marrow transplants are possible (http://www.nlm.nih.gov/medlineplus/ency/article/003009.htm, May 21, 2011).

- Autologous bone marrow transplant. "Auto" means "self." With this technique, stem cells are taken from the patient before the patient receives chemotherapy or radiation treatment. After the chemotherapy or radiation is finished, the patient gets his or her stem cells back. Such a "rescue" transplant allows the patient to receive high doses of chemotherapy and radiation.

- Allogeneic bone marrow transplant. "Allo" means "other." With this technique, stem cells come from another person, who is called a donor. Donor stem cells come from the donor's bone marrow or blood.

- Umbilical cord blood transplant. With this technique, stem cells are taken from an umbilical cord right after delivery of an infant. The stem cells are tested, typed, counted, and frozen until they are needed for a transplant. Umbilical cord blood requires less stringent matching because the stems cells are so immature.

The significance of bone marrow transplants as it relates to multiracials are the issues related to the donor of the bone marrow to the patient (Medline Plus 2011). Most times, a donor must have the same genetic typing as the patient, so that his or her blood "matches" the patient's blood. Special blood tests determine whether a possible donor is a good match for the patient. A patient's brothers and sisters have the highest chance of being a good match (25% chance for each full sibling), but sometimes parents and children of the patient and other relatives may be matches. Donors who are not related to the patient may be found through national bone marrow registries (http://www.nlm.nih.gov/medlineplus/ency/article/003009.htm, May 21, 2011). Only 30 percent of patients find matching donors within their families; the remaining 70 percent must search for an unrelated donor.

According to the Mixed Marrow Organization (2011), currently minorities make up only 30 percent of the registry, and only 2 percent of those persons registered are mixed race. Because not all mixes are the same combination, the actual odds of a mixed-race patient finding a match are lower than 2 percent. Moreover, race and ethnicity play an important role because six antigens (markers on the cells) must line up between the patient and the donor to create a perfect match. These antigens are inherited, so a match is more likely if the donor comes from a similar ethnic background.

What is so unfortunate and frightening about this situation for multiracials is that they consistently struggle to find bone marrow donors. While 6.8 million people identified themselves as multiracial in 2000 U.S. Census, only a tiny fraction of them are among the millions of registered bone marrow donors. For that reason, a Caucasian lymphoma patient who needs a bone marrow transplant has an almost 90 percent chance of finding a genetically compatible donor, while multiracial patients have little to no chance (Hernandez 2010).

PROBLEMS WITH FINDING DONORS

According to *Transplant News* (2009), the number of people who identify themselves as multiracial in the United States grew from 3.9 million in 2000 (the first year the census included the category) to 5.2 million in 2008. Mixed-race people account for 1.6 percent of the total U.S. population. Although the donor program has been pushing for years to recruit more racial minorities and mixed-race donors, multiracial volunteers so far make up just 3 percent of the 7 million people in the registry.

As explained by *Transplant News* (2009), the reason that mixed-heritage patients are so hard to match can be found in the immune system. Populations in different parts of the world developed certain proteins, or markers, that are part of the body's natural defenses. These markers help the immune system determine which cells are foreign and should be rejected. Because certain markers tend to cluster in particular ethnic groups, matches are most often found among people of shared backgrounds. Multiracial patients often have uncommon profiles and a much harder time finding a donor. Finding compatible organs for transplant is simpler because organ matches rely on blood type, which is unrelated to race (*Transplant News* 2009).

Multiracials in the United States are not alone in their challenge in finding appropriate bone marrow donors. Globally, there is a major disparity in the number of appropriate bone marrow donors for multiracials. According to *British National Party Newsroom* (2010), new reports that have focused on the problems surrounding suitable matches for bone marrow transplant patients have inadvertently revealed why an individual's racial background is significant factor. The *British National Party Newsroom* (2010) statistics revealed the following major findings:

1. White British people have a 1 in 3 likelihood of finding a bone marrow transplant match.

2. Asian or black people living in Britain have a 1 in 125,000 likelihood of finding a bone marrow transplant match.

3. People of mixed race living in Britain have a 1 in 200,000 or more likelihood of finding a bone marrow transplant match.

4. There are 16.9 million people on the National Health Service Organ Donor Register. Of this number, only 1.2 percent are Asian and 0.4 percent are black.
5. There are 7,800 patients currently waiting for a transplant in the United Kingdom, of whom 1,521 (19.5%) are Asian and 779 (9.98%) are black.

These statistics are significant because they reveal that not only do racial groups have different attitudes toward organ donation, but also that race is a major factor in determining diversity. For example, *British National Party Newsroom* (2010: 1) states that "transplanted organs require the same blood and tissue type in order to prevent rejection by the body's immune system." However, compared to organ transplants, bone marrow donations need to be even more genetically similar to their recipients. Because all the immune system's cells come from bone marrow, a transplant actually introduces a new immune system into a person. Without genetic similarity between the donor and the patient, the new white blood cells will attack the host's own cells (*British National Party Newsroom* 2010).

According to the National Marrow Donor Program's Be the Match Registry (2011), the chances of a Caucasian person finding a match with his or her specific racial group is 2 out of 3, while members of other racial groups have a 1 in 4 chance. The chances of a person of mixed racial origin finding a match, however, is even less because of the complex genetic issues involved. As a consequence, people of mixed racial origin in need of major organ transplants have almost no chance of finding an exact match even in highly mixed societies in which the gene pool is very intertwined (*British National Party Newsroom* 2010).

SPECIFIC EXAMPLE: NICK GLASGOW

Nick Glasgow passed away on October 6, 2009, from a long battle with leukemia. He was a 28-year-old employee of EMC Corporation in Pleasanton, California, who had mixed heritage: one-fourth Japanese and three-fourths Caucasian. Nick's condition drew global attention and support not only to the need for more potential bone marrow donors but also to people with mixed-race backgrounds.

In Nick's case, his grandfather, an Army soldier from South Carolina, fell in love with a Japanese woman while stationed in Japan after World War II and married across racial lines at time when it was illegal to do so in many states. Thus Nick's mixed heritage presented a major challenge for doctors to find a perfect match for his bone marrow transplant.

Inspired by Nick's story, thousands of people registered to be donors, first among his work colleagues at the corporation and then to the company's worldwide employees and beyond (CBS News 2009). Numerous articles and media outlets highlighted his plight in trying to find an appropriate donor for his bone marrow transplant. After his doctor found two perfect matches, Nick received a successful transplant in August 2009 and he was briefly cancer-free as he recovered from the effects of his difficult disease and treatment (Fredrickson 2009).

To document the struggle that Nick Glasgow, his mother, and the rest of his family experienced during this time period, a blog was created by a close friend who worked at the same company as Nick did. The name of his blog was "The Race to Save Nick Glasgow." From June 15, 2009, to October 15, 2009, the blog described specifically the day-to-day struggle by Nick, which unfortunately ended with his passing.

Nick Glasgow's story illustrates the challenges facing multiracials, their families, and friends when a serious medical and health situation such as leukemia requiring a bone marrow transplant strikes their lives. These are situations that many more Americans are experiencing each year. Therefore, it is increasingly important for everyone, but especially those persons of mixed heritage and ethnic backgrounds, to support programs and get tested as potential bone marrow donors.

DEVELOPING SOLUTIONS

In an effort to develop solutions for multiracials seeking a bone marrow transplant, a website, along with special bone marrow drives featuring another multiracial person (4-year-old Devan), was created. The Match-Devan site, which was launched in May 2010, became the focus of an unusual international campaign that attracted Hollywood celebrities, Internet entrepreneurs, and television reporters on behalf of the little boy who was battling a recurrence of acute promyelocytic leukemia.

Within the first week after the MatchDevan site went up, it received an estimated 80,000 visitors from 174 countries. Friends had also scheduled more than a dozen bone marrow drives in the United States and United Kingdom. Boodman (2010: 4) states that "the campaign attracted the attention of celebrities Ashton Kutcher and Kim Kardashian; Craig Newmark, founder of Craigslist; and television reporters Ann Curry and Andrea Mitchell who spread Devan's story to their millions of Twitter followers." More than 560 people registered as donors (Boodman 2010).

The chances of finding a perfectly matched donor were not merely distant for Devan—they were minuscule. The reason was his ethnic background: Devan is one-fourth South Asian and three-fourths Caucasian. Because matches are based on inherited tissue markers called human leukocyte antigens (HLAs), of which there are believed to be 5 million, some of them very rare, a donor is much more likely to come from the same racial or ethnic group as the recipient (Boodman 2010).

Despite the odds, Devan and his family are still fighting for all who need a fully matched bone marrow transplant. MatchDevan has been very successful in educating and raising awareness of bone marrow donation and organizing a bone marrow drive, and its Facebook page adds another successful media outlet to get the word out.

Another organization that started with a cause but has since become the lead advocacy organization for all types of causes for multiracials is the MAVIN Foundation. The MAVIN Foundation helps build healthier communities by raising awareness about the experience of mixed-heritage people and families (Stevens 2002). Since its humble start at a Connecticut university, to the launching of its national magazine dedicated to the "mixed-race experience," this group has focused attention on Matt Kelley, a 19-year-old freshman at Connecticut's Wesleyan University. The group quickly turned its spotlight to other multiracials, however. The MAVIN Foundation, led by two MAVIN Foundation interns, Yasmine Tarhouni and Justin Neiman, conducted MAVIN's first bone marrow drive in response to a Seattle biracial girl's fight against leukemia in 2001. Its efforts also laid the groundwork for MAVIN Foundation's MatchMaker Bone Marrow Project (www.mavinfoundation.org).

MatchMaker Bone Marrow started holding bone marrow donor recruitment drives in the Puget Sound region and then expanded nationally. It now works with local centers, recruitment groups, and the National Marrow Donor Program (NMDP) to address the chronic shortage of multiracial donors in the NMDP (www.mavinfoundation.org).

In 2002, the MatchMaker Bone Marrow project teamed up with students at Syracuse University (the university's Multiracial Experience organization and Phi Sigma Pi) along with 30 other college campuses for a Marrow-Thon, in which college students were encouraged to donate bone marrow to help those in need of marrow transplants, particularly people of mixed races. Marrow-Thon is important because people of mixed races donate the bone marrow. MatchMaker Bone Marrow has hosted more than 100 bone marrow events and registered a significant number of people, particularly those of mixed races.

CONCLUSION

Just a few years ago, bone marrow transplants were a very rare occurrence for most people. Most Americans heard about bone marrow transplants only when a local medical story was elevated by the national media, and a hunt for a potential bone marrow donor became national news.

The issues associated with bone marrow transplants present greater challenges for multiracials than for persons of a single race. Multiracials and other racial and ethnic populations are placed in a very precarious situation primarily because there are not enough bone marrow donors, and the bone marrow samples in the national registry are not diverse enough, particularly for people of mixed heritage.

According to Dr. Laurence Cooper, Associate Professor of Pediatrics at the Children's Cancer Hospital at the University of Texas M. D. Anderson Cancer Center, there are three major strategies for patients who are challenged in finding a donor:

- We want people to donate who are from minority groups and who have mixed parenting. They are a special pool and could give to other people who are like themselves. If you could get more potential donors out there, you could essentially enjoy the same benefits as Caucasians.

- The second answer is we want people to donate their cord blood. If more people donate their cord blood, the chances of us finding a near-miss go up. It doesn't have to be perfect. We can find a nearly HLA identical child who has given up his or her cord blood at the time of birth.

- We continue to develop new technology to overcome [these] issues where we can develop transplants for special groups [using] donors that are HLA mismatched, but [we can] do special maneuvers. (Hernandez 2010)

These are strategies that many clinicians and scholars (Bergstrom, Garratt, and Sheehan-Conner 2011) support and are at the forefront in changing how people and organizations of all different racial and ethnic affiliations and background view bone marrow transplants among multiracials.

NINE

Multiracials and Transracial Adoption

INTRODUCTION

This issue of transracial adoption came to my attention when I was an assistant professor at Indiana University at Indianapolis from 1990 to 1997. As an assistant professor in the Department of Anthropology, I realized that this position and appointment was somewhat ground-breaking simply because there were very few persons of color employed as faculty members in the College of Arts and Sciences, and even very few professional persons of color affiliated with the university.

After a few months in the position, I was approached by one of the senior (Caucasian) faculty members in the college. He wanted my insight into understanding some issues his young son was experiencing. Because his young, adopted son was African American, he naturally felt that I could share some cultural information that he and his wife were not aware of, which could help in the raising of their son.

The major issues I recall that this senior Caucasian faculty member faced with his adopted African American son involved his son's desire to connect with someone in his age group who looked like him, and his desire for his parents to understand some of the discriminatory situations that he was experiencing at school. This was a major challenge for this very empathetic, caring, and liberal-minded faculty member. But it was uncharted territory that he and his wife had to venture into, for the well-being of their son.

The primary purpose of sharing that experience with transracial adoption is to show that parents have to be aware of multiple sociocultural, ethnic, and individual issues when considering transracial adoption of children of all backgrounds, but particularly multiracials. This early experience with transracial adoption issues also informed my concern regarding this seriously overlooked, and often hidden, issue that many families and children have experienced in the past, and that they continue to experience today. Highlighting this issue may provide a new appreciation, understanding, and direction for dealing with some major issues that multiracial adoptees and families may face in 2012 and beyond.

BACKGROUND

Transracial adoption—meaning the placement of children for adoption across racial lines—has received much attention in the public and in legislation during the past few decades. According to McRoy and Hall (1996), this definition seems to imply that all types of American children might be placed with families who are of a different racial background than the children. In reality, the term *transracial adoption* typically refers to the one-way transfer of children of color into white families (McRoy and Hall 1996: 64).

Historically, the public child welfare system was designed to find adoptive homes for white infants and babies for childless couples, at least since the 1920s. Until the mid-1960s, adoptions were viewed as a "white middle-class affair," as the majority of the clientele at private adoption agencies were white middle- and upper-income families (Morgentern 1971). In fact, in many states, adoption across racial lines was prohibited (McRoy and Hall 1996). It was not until 1967 in Texas and 1972 in Louisiana that the last two state statutes denying adoption across racial lines were ruled unconstitutional.

In the 1960s, private adoption agencies experienced a significant decline in the number of healthy white infants available for adoption, due to the widespread use of contraceptives, availability of abortions, and lessening of the stigma toward unwed parenthood. Along with the new focus on integration in the 1960s and the need for more infants to place with prospective white adoptive families, some agencies began to advocate for transracial placements. In 1971, approximately 2,500 black children were placed transracially (Simon 1984).

In opposition to this practice, in 1972 the National Association of Black Social Workers (NABSW) issued a resolution that called for the cessation of transracial placements, asserting that "black children in white homes are cut off from the healthy development of themselves as black people" (McRoy and Hall 1996: 64). This position statement influenced agency practice between 1972 and 1975, causing the overall number of transracial replacements to significantly decline and the number of in-racial adoptions of black children to increase (McRoy and Zurcher 1983).

The following year, the Child Welfare League of America revised its standards for adoption practice and acknowledged that in-racial placements are preferable because children placed in adoptive families with similar distinctive characteristics can become more easily integrated into the average family and community (McRoy and Hall 1996: 66). Nevertheless, as the number of white infants and young children available for adoption continued to decrease and the number of white families wanting to adopt increased, agencies gradually resumed transracial placements. The National Council for Adoption estimated that approximately 25,000 infants younger than 2 years of age were placed for adoption in 1986 (McRoy and Hall 1996).

McRoy and Hall (1996) explain that another phenomenon influencing transracial adoption during the period was the growing number of children in foster care. In 1986, 273,000 children were in out-of-home care. In large part to the drug epidemic as well as an economic decline in the mid-1980s, 360,000 children were in foster care by 1989. By 1992, that number had risen to 450,000. Children of color were overrepresented in these statistics, and in many states more than half of the children needing placement were African American.

As the number of African American children needing out-of-home placement exceeded the number of available African American foster families, these children were often placed in transracial foster care. Many children remained with these families, often separated from their siblings, with limited contact with their birth families or extended families for several years before they were either returned to their birth families or placed in adoption. In a number of cases, however, white foster families sought to adopt black children whom they had fostered since infancy, thereby increasing the rates of transracial adoption (McRoy and Hill 1996).

In 1994, the federal government became a major player in the debate over transracial adoption. "[W]hen Senator Howard Metzenbaum, of Ohio, initially introduced the Multiethnic Ethnic Placement Act in a Floor Statement on July 15, 1993, he spoke of a white couple in Arizona seeking to adopt their 3-year-old black foster daughter, who had lived with them since the age of 3 months" (McRoy and Hill 1996: 70). Metzenbaum also spoke of a biracial couple in Minnesota who had been forced to give up their 4-year-old black foster son, whom they were trying to adopt. The senator stated that something must be done to help these and other children who were being denied the opportunity to be part of a stable and caring family, when a same-race family was not available. Passed in 1994, the ensuing legislation prohibited the denial of a placement solely on the basis of race but allowed for consideration of the cultural, ethnic, or racial background of the child and the capacity of the prospective foster parents to meet the needs of a child of this background. McRoy and Hill (1996) concluded that the fact that this legislation was needed is fascinating because historically race has always been a major consideration in the placement of white children with white families.

Transracial adoption remains a very highly socially, politically, and culturally charged issue. Whether it was 5, 10, 20, or 30 years ago, transracial adoption was a highly controversial topic, and it continues to engender debate today. This is a system that supposed to place children of all different racial and ethnic backgrounds with families of all different racial and ethnic backgrounds. Yet in our American system of transracial adoption, it nearly always means the one-way transfer of children of color to white families. Why is this a cultural pattern, and are American families prepared for the rapid increase in transracial adoptions to come?

PERSONAL ACCOUNTS OF TRANSRACIAL ADOPTION

Parents' Perspective

Although few accounts have documented the parents' perspective on transracial adoption and the issues surrounding transracial families, there have recently been a few in-depth articles and blogs that have captured their plight with remarkable sensitivity. An article entitled "Transracial Adoption Leads to Stares: How One Mother Deals" (Ruby 2010) noted that transracial families are still new to most Americans; unfortunately, as recounted in this article, staring from others continues to occur during public encounters with such families.

The author of this article, Lilly Ruby, a Caucasian female, recalled her early days after adopting multiracial children. When her children first came home; people looked at them whenever they went to a water park, mall, the grocery store, the train station, or the beach. During their first summer as a family, people appeared to be captivated by the striking beauty of her eldest, the dark shade of her skin made even more apparent in the summer sun (Ruby 2010).

Frequently, the family received stares when they went to restaurants. Ruby (2010) recalled that at one dinner in particular, the family behind them was staring at her daughter, with two little girls whispering about Ruby's family. While her daughter tried to ignore the unwanted attention,

Ruby recalled that the incident hurt her own heart. Eventually, Ruby leaned over the booth and politely waved at the staring family.

Months later after this incident, the same thing happened again in the same restaurant. Ruby had returned from taking her toddler to the restroom when her eldest child reported that the people at the facing table were staring at her. This time, Ruby told her eldest to smile and wave. She did, and then Ruby turned around and smiled and politely waved at them. They all waved and smiled back. The mother said, "Your kids are beautiful, and so well behaved." Ruby simply thanked her.

Two years later, Ruby (2010) said that she and her kids now ignore the staring, or perhaps they no longer notice it. She also has been made acutely aware that her personal repertoire of responses and reactions will continue to develop as she grows in her own understanding of her family and their place in the world. Furthermore, Ruby stated that her children's reactions will change as they move through varying development stages.

When asked if race gets in the way, Ruby (2010) notes that she does not know what her kids go through, but she encourages them to not let their negative experiences hurt their hearts. Thus, as a Caucasian woman who decided to adopt her multiracial children, Ruby concluded that she should let her children have their feelings, even though those feelings might be painful at times. She can help them speak their truth and help them to deal with whatever comes their way, but to grow, they must accept that "looking different" is a part of their lives and recognize that theirs is a real family built by adoption, bonded by love.

Ruby (2010) emphasizes that her children have a place where they belong and parents who love and adore them. This positive environment in their internal family setting appears to take the hurt out of things, she found. For all the questions and staring from strangers, the racial divide has in some ways strengthened the family. After all, when held up against the bond that they have—the humor, the connection, the trust, the love—nothing really stands a chance (Ruby 2010: 2).

Another personal account from a parent's perspective of transracial adoption comes from a multiracial family blog posting an article entitled "Transracial Adoption: It Will Change Your Family Forever." The article starts as follows:

As a white person, my understanding of what it took to bring a black, Latino, or Asian child into my family was straightforward. You either adopted a black or biracial child domestically or you traveled to Guatemala, Colombia, Ethiopia or somewhere in Asia to bring a child of color home. You made sure that your child had role models within her race and you incorporated the holidays and traditions of your child's family of origin into the life of your family. You joined a support group for people with families like yours so that your child could make friends with others of her race and you could share advice and support. (Berger 2010: 1)

For Berger (2010), however, her early thoughts about transracial adoption barely scratched the surface of the reality of such adoptions. Many white preadoptive parents contend that they are prepared to adopt transracially, she notes, because they are comfortable with people of color. But, Berger stresses, we must look at life through the children's eyes. As Berger (2010) emphasizes, the children who are adopted across racial lines will be living in a society that is not yet fully comfortable with race nor color blind.

In fact, transracial adoption by whites has continued to significantly increase. In 2004, Clemetson and Nixon (2006) noted that "of children who were adopted before the age of 18, 16% were black, 7% were Asian and 2% were American Indian." Of these children, 17 percent were of a different race than their adoptive parents. In addition, transracial adoption through foster care is on the rise. In 2004, 26 percent of black children were adopted transracially, almost always by whites, compared to 14 percent in 1998 (Clemetson and Nixon 2006).

There are many children of color both in the United States and abroad who are in need of families, and there are many white couples and individuals who want to provide homes for these children. The question is not whether families should adopt transracially, but rather how they can do a better job of it. What this means is that we have to think differently about raising children of other races.

Berger (2010) offers several general suggestions for those couples who want to do a better job in parenting multiracial children. The most important step, she notes, is to make friends among members of your child's race and open yourself to discussions about race. This will allow white adoptive parents to discover that they may have never had such discussions, as this subject is generally considered taboo.

Berger's (2010) next piece of advice is for parents to realize that the *transracialization* of the family will be an ongoing, endless, rewarding, frustrating, and exciting experience that will affect future generations. Complete transracialization is not always achieved by white adoptive families, yet we need to strive for it if we want our children to develop healthy identities (Berger 2010).

Finally, Berger (2010: 3) suggests that there are many things that white adoptive parents of multiracial children can do to improve the experiences of both parents and children:

- Live in a diverse community where there are many people of your child's race.
- Ensure that your child attends a racially diverse school.
- Educate your extended family regarding your child's race and culture.
- Find same-race role models and mentors for your child.
- Learn to speak your child's language of origin.
- Select vacation places and camps where your child's race is well represented.
- Attend social and cultural events similar to those attended by members of your child's race.
- Address racism and confront it together.
- Include the music, food, and holiday traditions of your child's race into your family life.

Multiracial Children's/Adults' Perspective

Now that we have a sense of the major social and cultural issues related to transracial parents' (primarily Caucasian parents') perceptions of the transracial adoption process, or the transracialization of their family, let us consider some of the major social and cultural issues related to multiracial adults who lived with transracial families when they were children. In an innovative research study and article entitled "Being Raised by White People: Navigating Racial Difference among Adopted Multiracial Adults," Samuels (2009) presents findings from an extended case method (ECM) study of 25 adult black-white multiracials, using in-depth interviews to explore their developmental experiences of race, culture, and kinship.

According to Samuels (2009), the ECM is a hybrid case-based method that produces ecologically nested findings to extend existing conceptualizations or theories. As a scientific theory, it draws from both social constructivist and critical traditions, requiring multisystemic analyses of a unique case. Basically, emic (personal) perspectives and experiences are analyzed to better understand the individual's perspective. In Samuels' (2009: 83) work, "this analysis produced three broad patterns of identity work among the participants in this study which involved being raised by white families, searching for kinship, and recognizing one's identity." Overall, his study helped to answer one major question: *What's it like being raised by white people?*

To obtain data from this particular segment of the population, Samuel (2009) used recruitment methods, including print and web-based advertisements across the United States, directed toward African American, multiracial, and transracial adoption organizations and agencies; brochures and magazines; mailings to college student groups and adoption networks; and word of mouth. Criteria for inclusion in the study included a minimum age of 18 and a black-white heritage with white adoptive parents.

Participants in the study were audiotaped during in-depth interviews lasting approximately 2 hours. All interviews were conducted by Samuels, and the data were analyzed with the latest computer software.

Samuels (2009) started the interviews by asking participants to share their adoption stories, including what they knew about their birth families. Participants described what their childhood communities were like, how they were raised to think about their racial heritages and adoptions, and whether their insights or identities changed as they became adults. Participants shared their stories of searching for biological families, experiencing racism and prejudice inside their adoptive and biological family systems, and parsing the meaning of multiraciality and transracial adoption in both black and white communities. The interviews ended with the participants sharing advice for adopted persons, parents, and adoption professionals. Samuels is himself multiracial and transracially adopted (84).

According to Samuels (2009), when assessing his study results, it is important to recognize that participants conveyed both the advantages and the disadvantages of their adoptions. They often used words such as "opportunities" to describe how transracial adoption enhanced their lives. All mentioned advantages linked to success in mainstream contexts and noted travel, access to "good" education, and their middle- to upper-middle-class status as being among the positive benefits. They frequently attributed being "worldly" and racially "open-minded" to their multiracial and transracial adoptive backgrounds.

Samuels (2009) highlights the words of participant Sheila, age 30, who stated:

I feel like I have this HUGE gift to relate to people to both worlds. Nobody getting over on me. I feel it's my job to educate . . . Sometimes I feel like that's my mission in life. Everywhere I go. (85)

Samuels (2009) notes that all participants' stories of growing up portrayed how their early feelings of difference became racialized and consumed by navigating problems between their lived experiences of race and that of others. For example, although a multiracial adopted child's white heritage might help some white parents feel connected to the child, it does not facilitate a mutual racial connection or shared racial experience for the child. Instead, it supports a feeling of distinct racial complexity.

Samuel's (2009) study also found that the physical appearance of the adopted child is important to his or her successful adaptation to the new surroundings. For example, participant Sheila felt disconnected from her adoptive family because they did not look like her racially. This caused her to question her parents' insight. In contrast, participant Todd emphasized that his physical appearance helped him to blend in racially with the parents of his black friends, which he felt it was impossible to do with his white parents. In effect, this interaction offered an important respite for Todd (87).

Overall, according to Samuels (2009), the stories of race and family among his participants encompassed many layers of psychosociocultural issues. Their understandings of race and adoption were inseparable from their experiencing of race as multiracial individuals growing up in white adoptive families. These were lifetime identities. The few participants who felt their parents were helpful ($n = 5$) saw them as joining on a journey, challenging themselves to see the world through their child's multiracial eyes. This attitude reduced participants' felt disconnection even into adulthood. Parents were viewed as supportive when they were present in their child's racialized world across the life course.

Samuels (2009) suggests that future research should include family-based longitudinal designs that encompass greater class diversity, drawing on the perspectives of all family members involved in the adoptive experiences over the life course. Additionally, recruiting families who transracially adopt children from foster care may yield more class-balanced samples.

Today's adopted multiracials have many more opportunities for connecting to these groups with a shared racial experience. Building relationships among children within these communities is important, not because all people must claim or find membership within these racial-ethnic groups, but rather because adults and peers from these communities represent additional sources of support, kinship, and affirmation (Samuels 2009: 93).

A NEW MODEL FOR UNDERSTANDING AND SOLVING TRANSRACIAL ADOPTION ISSUES

In 2013, it seems that more and more new community groups and organizations are forming across the United States, in major metropolitan areas, suburban areas, and rural areas, focusing their mission and resources on assisting individuals and families with transracial adoption issues. Because the changing face of the American family includes individuals of mixed racial, ethnic, and cultural heritages, and because the numbers of such persons have dramatically increased in the past few decades, there is a need to develop a new model, or framework, for professionals who are willing to work with these families and their unique issues. That is why there is now a major movement within various professional fields (human services and counseling, family therapy, psychology, and social work) to operationalize a new model.

One such model is the Cultural-Racial Identity Model. Developed by Steward and Baden (1995), this model seeks to address the compelling roles of both race and culture within families where racial homogeneity does not necessarily exist.

The Cultural-Racial Identity Model can serve as a framework for understanding and working with members of racially integrated families for two reasons. First, it accounts for racial and cultural differences among parents and their children. Second, the model takes into consideration the impact that the experiences and the attitudes of their parents, peers, extended family, social support networks, and the larger community have on the children. For these reasons, Baden and Steward (2000) contend, the Cultural-Racial Identity Model is both a comprehensive and a current framework for use with racially integrated families.

Basically, the Cultural-Racial Identity Model consists of two axes: the Cultural Identity Axis and the Racial Identity Axis. The final model combines these two axes into a single model (Baden and Steward 2000).

In the case of transracial adoptees, the adoptees are from a different racial group than their adoptive parents. Thus, at least two different racial groups, as well as two different cultures, can be represented within transracially adopting families. For this reason, Steward and Baden (1995) developed the Cultural-Identity Axis to represent four possible combinations of cultural endorsements. It features two dimensions:

1. Adoptee Culture Dimension—the degree to which transracial adoptees identify with their own racial group's culture (e.g., if the adoptee is Korean, the degree to which the adoptee identifies with Korean culture).

2. Parental Culture Dimension—the degree to which transracial adopt-ees identify with the culture of their adoptive parents' racial group (e.g., because most transracially adopting parents are white, the degree to which the adoptee identifies with white culture).

Baden and Steward (2000: 324) contend that "the transracial adoptees' level of identification with a culture or cultures is determined by their lev-els of knowledge, awareness, competence, and comfort with either or both the culture of their own racial group, their parents' racial group, or multi-ple racial groups." Four types of cultural identities—Bicultural Identity, Pro-Self Cultural Identity, Pro-Parent Cultural Identity, and Culturally Undifferentiated Identity—exist according to this model, with each differ-ing according to level of the transracial adoptee on each of the two dimen-sions along the Cultural-Identity Axis.

For example, transracial adoptees identifying more highly with the culture of their adoptive parents' racial group (i.e., the white culture) would be high on the Parental Culture Dimension and low on the Adoptees' Culture Dimension; thus the adoptees would have Pro-Parent Cultural Identities. Transracial adoptees who identify with the culture traditionally associated with their birth culture and who simultaneously feel less comfortable with the culture of their adoptive parents would be low on the Parental Culture Dimension and high on the Adoptees' Culture Dimension; thus they would have Pro-Self Cultural Identities.

In transracially adopting families, racial differences also exist among family members, which moved Steward and Baden (1995) to develop the Racial Identity Axis in the Cultural-Racial Identity Model. The Racial Identity Axis has two dimensions:

1. Adoptee Race Dimension—the degree to which transracial adoptees identify with their own racial group (e.g., if the adoptee is black, the degree to which the adoptee identifies with blacks).

2. Parental Race Dimension—the degree to which transracial adoptees identify with their adoptive parents' racial group (e.g., because most transracially adopting parents are white, the degree to which the adoptee identifies with whites).

Transracial adoptees' levels of identification with a racial group are determined by assessing the degree to which the adoptees self-identify as belonging to their own racial group or to their parents' racial group. Four possible racial identities are possible: Biracial Identity, Pro-Self

Racial Identity, Pro-Parent Racial Identity, and Racially Undifferentiated (Baden and Steward 2000: 327).

The final model combines the Cultural Identity Axis and the Racial Identity Axis into a single model. Baden and Steward (2000: 324) emphasize that "the Cultural-Racial Identity Model represents the pairing of each of the four types of possible cultural identities." The resulting model has 16 identity statuses that can be used to describe the identities of transracial adoptees:

1. Pro-Self Cultural Identity—Pro-Self Racial Identity
2. Pro-Self Cultural Identity—Biracial Identity
3. Pro-Self Cultural Identity—Racially Undifferentiated Identity
4. Pro-Self Cultural Identity—Pro-Parent Racial Identity
5. Culturally Undifferentiated—Pro-Self Racial Identity
6. Culturally Undifferentiated—Biracial Identity
7. Culturally Undifferentiated—Racially Undifferentiated Identity
8. Culturally Undifferentiated—Pro-Parent Racial Identity
9. Bicultural—Pro-Self Racial Identity
10. Bicultural—Biracial Identity
11. Bicultural—Racially Undifferentiated Identity
12. Bicultural—Pro-Parent Racial Identity
13. Pro-Parent Cultural Identity—Pro-Self Racial Identity
14. Pro-Parent Cultural Identity—Biracial Identity
15. Pro-Parent Cultural Identity—Racially Undifferentiated Identity
16. Pro-Parent Cultural Identity—Pro-Parent Racial Identity (Baden and Steward 2000)

Summarizing their work, Baden and Steward (2000: 334) note that "the Cultural-Racial Identity Model was the first theoretical model to separate cultural identity and racial identity." The implications for its use are vast and point to the need for the empirical validation of the model. This model can serve as a guide for transracial adoptees and adoptive parents to better understand and guide their life experiences. Moreover, psychotherapeutic practitioners can use the model as a guide for determining the counseling needs of those persons raised in racially integrated families, particularly as they differ from the needs of individuals raised in same-race households.

Before all of this happens, however, empirical evidence must be gathered that support the Cultural-Racial Identity Model. Cases need to be tested in all types of clinical, public, and community-based settings, and data need to be collected both quantitatively and qualitatively. Once this occurs, then the information gathered from the application of the Cultural-Racial Identity Model to groups such as transracial adoptees and biracial individuals can be put to work in practice. In turn, psychologists, social workers, adoption workers, and others in the health professions will be better prepared to address the adjustment, identity, and esteem problems that have been of such concern to opponents and proponents of transracial adoption alike (Baden and Steward 2000: 335).

CONCLUSION

Transracial adoption is a growing trend among multiracial children. Transracial adoption is no longer considered an oddity, or even a very rare occurrence. Celebrity couple Brad Pitt and Angelina Jolie have brought international attention to the issues associated with transracial adoption and multiracial children (Pax Thien, Shiloh Nouvel, Zahara Marley, and Maddox Chivan); they are a prime example of individuals making these decisions because they simply feel a strong desire to raise, nurture, and help children, regardless of their multiracial background. Tom Cruise, his ex-wife Nicole Kidman, and their adopted multiracial son Connor have also drawn international attention to transracial adoption in recent years.

Transracial adoption is here to stay, and is finally getting the necessary assistance to support it on a long-term basis from a wide variety of organizations and groups. Groups such as Multiracial Sky (www.multiracialsky .com) and Open Arms Adoption (www.openarmsadoption.com) are leading the way for individuals and families who are ready to adopt outside of their socially designated racial group. This is a very significant step for mainstream America, and particularly for ethnic-specific racial groups in the United States. It is getting all of us prepared for another level of race relations and transracialization.

PART IV

Future Trends

TEN

Multiracial Celebrities: Leading America to the Next Century

INTRODUCTION

Multiracial Americans have contributed to all facets of life in the United States since its earliest beginnings. In fact, multiracial Americans are not just contributing to our country—they are leading America into the 21st century in more ways than the average American could ever imagine.

Although many of these pioneering individuals have had to label themselves in one of the traditional U.S. racial and ethnic categories, more and more are deciding individually to acknowledge their multiracial ethnic backgrounds. This public acknowledgment not only helps multiracials' numbers census-wise, but more importantly sends a cultural message, loud and clear, that multiracial Americans should be seen as role models and leaders and truly be recognized for their contributions (Multiracial Heritage Week 2011).

This chapter highlights a selected group of multiracial celebrities who have shown the world that they are truly uniquely talented and effective at what they do. Some are individuals who regularly acknowledge their multiracial identity; others do not. Yet irrespective of their acknowledgment of their multiracial identity, the world sees and perceives them differently depending upon their racial and ethnic background. This is one reason why these multiracial celebrities connect with so many different racial and ethnic groups. They connect visually and culturally with a wide variety of audiences, because these audiences feel that they are "one of them." As a consequence, these multiracial celebrities (movie, sports, news, and political) may have especially loyal followings of fans and supporters.

MOVIE CELEBRITIES

One of Americans' favorite pastimes has always been going to the movies. Ever since films were created and mass-produced, Americans from all walks of life have attended showings at movie theaters, hoping to watch a film that would make them laugh, move them emotionally, or help them dream the impossible dream. Whatever the reason that compels droves of folks to attend movies each year, the actors and actresses in movies have inspired, and oftentimes become a reflection of, their audiences.

Now that audiences can see a movie in many different ways—at the movie theater, by renting a DVD/Blu-ray Disc, or by downloading it from an online source—the movies, along with the actors and actresses who appear in them, seem more accessible than ever before. This perceived accessibility allows audiences of all types to better connect with the new genre of actresses and actors.

These new leading actors and actresses include Vin Diesel, Natalie Portman, Keanu Reeves, Dwayne Johnson, Rosario Dawson, Cameron Diaz, and Rashida Jones. These actresses and actors are multiracial. They are making blockbuster movies and are on the "A list" for Hollywood's promotional movie machine. They are leading the movie industry in a new direction for the new century. To recognize the contributions of these multiracial celebrities, this chapter highlights some of them who are making a difference.

Vin Diesel

The name "Vin Diesel" invokes an image of physicality, and often sparks an interest in who the actor is. Vin Diesel has Italian and African American heritage. When I first saw Diesel (actual name: Mark Sinclair Vincent), he was the lead actor in the moderate-budget science fiction movie called *Pitch Black* (2000). This sci-fi movie depicted the outcast character (role: Richard B. Riddick) as a mysterious, physical, unpredictable antihero. His casting and the moderate box office success of *Pitch Black* helped Diesel to land his biggest mainstream movie at the time—*The Fast and the Furious* (2001).

The blockbuster success of *The Fast and the Furious* propelled Diesel into stardom as an action hero. Not only was his acting serious, real, in-depth, and street-wise, but his physical, muscular appearance appealed to women and men of all types of racial and ethnic backgrounds. Although many racial and ethnic audiences related to him, it was Diesel's appeal to mainstream movie audiences that surprised many movie critics (Beltran 2005). Many mainstream movie audience members were looking for a lead actor who was different than the norm, not your typical-looking Hollywood leading man; Vin Diesel fit that bill.

Other movie credits for this actor included *Saving Private Ryan* (1998), *The Iron Giant* (1999), *xXx* (2002), *The Chronicles of Riddick* (2004), *The Pacifier* (2005), *Find Me Guilty* (2005), *The Fast and the Furious: Tokyo Drift* (2006), and *Babylon A.D.* (2008). With the success of each movie, Diesel became more established as a bankable leading actor in mainstream moviegoer theaters. In 2011, his movie *The Fast Five*, which opened at number 1 domestically and internationally, proved to movie critics that not only did Diesel have appeal to American audiences, but he also had an international appeal that very few actors could match (www.vindiesel.com, accessed June 5, 2011).

Diesel also sets himself apart from many typical Hollywood actors by always showing commitment to his roots through his One Race Global Foundation. The One Race Global Foundation is a nonprofit organization that attempts to foster diverse voices in underserved communities through education and training in film and video production (www.causes.com/causes/351503). Because the actor himself had challenging experiences in making his own films when he first started in the film industry, he has established the One Race Global Film Foundation to provide opportunities for the next generation of diverse, underserved youths interested in film making.

Diesel's 1994 short film titled *Multi-Facial* is a semi-autobiographical film that follows a struggling biracial actor. In this film, which he produced, directed, and acted in, Diesel shows how racism, discrimination, and stereotyping infiltrate our perceptions and affecs decisions on some of the most basic issues associated with race and race relations.

Natalie Portman

One of the most internationally well-known young actresses of our times and the Academy Award winner for best actress in the 2010 film *Black Swan*, Natalie Portman has steadily acted in movies since 1994. When I first saw Natalie Portman in the movies, she starred in one of the biggest franchise movies of all time—the *Stars Wars* "prequels." Playing a key role in the movies as Padme Amidala (Queen Amidala), she immediately skyrocketed to *Star Wars* fame after being directed by the famous George Lucas. Now a veteran actress, Harvard graduate Portman has won high respect and honors from the Hollywood establishment, and she also receives high respect and honors from prestigious international organizations due to her charity work and her desire to learn more about world issues.

Born as Natalie Hershlag, Portman has dual American and Israeli citizenship—her mother is an American citizen and her father is an Israeli citizen. Portman's parents met at a Jewish student center at Ohio State University, where her mother was selling tickets. They kept in contact after her father returned to Israel, and were married when her mother visited a few years later. Natalie Portman was born in Jerusalem, Israel (http://www.natalieport man.com). Her movie credits include *The Professional* (1994), *Mars Attacks!* (1996), *Star Wars Episodes I, II, and III* (1999, 2002, 2005), *V for Vendetta* (2006), *Mr. Magorium's Wonder Emporium* (2007), *Black Swan* (2010), and *Thor* (2011), to name a few.

In particular, Portman's portrayal of Evey Hammond, a young woman who is protected from the secret police by the main character, V, in the movie *V for Vendetta* made both audiences and critics aware of her social and political stance. Portman has discussed *V for Vendetta*'s political relevance and mentioned that her character, who joins an underground antigovernment group, is "Often bad and does things that you don't like." She has also stated that "Being from Israel was a reason I wanted to do this because terrorism and violence are such a daily part of my conversations since I was little" (JoBlo.com 2006). Film critics say that the film did not make clear good or bad statements about a political government, but allowed the audience to draw their own conclusions.

As for Portman's charities and foundations, she supports numerous organizations. Here are a few of them (http://www.looktothestars.org/ celebrity/225-natalie-portman):

- Foundation for International Community Assistance (FINCA)
- Afghanistan Relief Organization
- Food Bank for New York City
- Shoe4Africa
- Listen Campaign
- Live 8
- People for Ethical Treatment for Animals (PETA)
- The Lunchbox Fund
- Tony Blair Faith Foundation

- Artists for Peace and Justice
- Milo Gladstein Foundation

In a *USA Today* article entitled "Natalie Portman Is Force for Change, Empowering Women," Freydkin (2008) stated that the Israeli American actress "gravitated toward FINCA because of her interest in the Middle East and a desire to collaborate with Jordan's Queen Rania Al-Abdullah, who chairs FINCA's Village Banking campaign." Yet before affiliating herself with this cause, Portman learned as much as possible by traveling to Guatemala with FINCA and then to Uganda and Ecuador. She recalled later:

In Guatemala, I remember seeing a family with four generations of women. It might have even been five. They were together, living together, and the grandmother was watching the baby while the women were in the market. They had a small food stand, and with a loan they were able to buy a scale. That vastly grew their business. They got a refrigerator. Whatever they didn't sell could keep for longer. (Freydkin 2008)

Another foundation with which Portman has strong ties is the Milo Gladstein Foundation. This organization was founded by Lauri and Richard Gladstein in 2004, shortly after their son Milo was diagnosed with Bloom's syndrome. The foundation's goal is to fund research aimed at the development of a therapy for Bloom's syndrome and the prevention of its complications, primarily the significant risk of developing cancers at early ages.

Bloom's syndrome is a very rare disorder in most populations, and its overall frequency is unknown. The National Library of Medicine (2013: 1) states that "the disorder is more common in people of Central and Eastern European (Ashkenazi) Jewish background, of which about 1 in 50,000 are affected." People with Bloom's syndrome are characterized by short stature, sun-sensitive skin change, increased risk of cancer, and other health problems (http://ghr.nlm.nih.gov/condition/bloom-syndrome).

One of the fundraising events for the Milo Gladstein Foundation was the Clothes Off Our Back campaign (www.clothesoffourback.org). In August 2006, Portman hosted an online auction in which she auctioned off autographed memorabilia from *Star Wars* and a gown she wore to a special event. Other well-known celebrities contributed personal items. One hundred percent of the proceeds from the auction went to the Bloom's Syndrome Foundation.

Portman's acting career, educational background, charitable work, and her personal familial background make it clear that she is a person who is focused, committed, and dedicated to helping others in improve their lives. Portman has shown that she is a leader and role model for numerous causes and organizations.

Dwayne Johnson ("The Rock")

Dwayne Johnson is another actor whose professional name makes us think action-oriented, physicality, toughness, muscles, great smile, and intensity. Originally known for his championship wrestling career in the World Wrestling Federation (WWF) as "The Rock," Johnson gradually parlayed his fame from wrestling into stardom in Hollywood.

Dwayne Johnson's heritage is diverse. His father is of black Nova Scotian (Canadian) origin, and his mother is of Samoan heritage. Born in Hayward, California, Johnson is the son of Ata Johnson and professional wrestler "Soulman" Rocky Johnson. Some years later, he lived in Auckland, New Zealand, with his mother's family to ensure that he was exposed to one of the urban Polynesian cultural strongholds of the Southern Hemisphere (http://www.facebook.com/DwayneJohnson). During his visit to Samoa in 2004, Johnson was given the noble title of *Seiulu* for his years of service to Samoan people. Because his mother Ata had royal blood, the Samoan king bestowed this honor.

Johnson was also a college football player who played for the University of Miami Hurricanes. In 1991, the team won a national championship. Later, Johnson played for the Calgary Stampede in the Canadian Football League.

After years playing "The Rock" with the World Wrestling Federation, Johnson gravitated toward acting. His movie credits include *The Mummy Returns* (2001), *The Scorpion King* (2002), *The Rundown* (2003), *Walking Tall* (2004), *Gridiron Gang* (2006), *Get Smart* (2008), *Race to Witch Mountain* (2009), *Tooth Fairy* (2009), *Faster* (2010), and *Fast Five* (2011).

Besides donating $2 million in 2006 to the University of Miami with his ex-wife Dany Garcia, Dwayne Johnson has engaged in widespread charity and foundation work. Here are a few of these endeavors (http://www .looktothestars.org/celebrity/549-dwayne-johnson):

- Dwayne Johnson Rock Foundation
- Beacon Experience
- I Have a Dream Foundation

- Make-a-Wish Foundation
- Make the Difference Network
- Parkinson Society Maritime Region
- Red Cross
- Rush Philanthropic Arts Foundation
- Starlight Children's Foundation
- Until There's a Cure

For example, his personal foundation—Dwayne Johnson Rock Foundation—not only strives to assist hospitalized children in their recovery process, but also assists children with education enrichment programs and childhood obesity prevention.

Dwayne Johnson is a multitalented actor, athlete, and humanitarian who recognizes his heritage while also helping those who are in need. It appears likely that Johnson will continue to use his worldwide celebrity status as an actor and ex-wrestler to create more opportunities for hope and improved quality of life for those in need.

Cameron Diaz

Former model and now internationally known actress Cameron Diaz has captured movie audiences since 1994, with her first major movie role in *The Mask*. Yet it was not until her role in another mega-movie, *There's Something about Mary*, that Diaz was propelled into wider fame.

Diaz has a diverse heritage, with her father's family coming from Cuba and her mother being of English, German, Native American, and Dutch descent. She was born and raised in California and started her modeling career at age 16 by contracting with the agency Elite Model Management. Diaz modeled internationally; in fact, when she was 17 years old, she was featured on the cover of the July 1990 issue of *Seventeen* magazine (http://www.cameron-diaz.com).

By age 21, Diaz had branched out from modeling; she took acting lessons and then started to land roles in major motion pictures. Her movie credits include *The Mask* (1994), *The Last Supper* (1995), *She's the One* (1995), *Feeling Minnesota* (1996), *My Best Friend's Wedding* (1997), *There's Something about Mary* (1998), *Being John Malkovich* (1999), *Any Given Sunday* (1999), *Charlie's Angels* (2000), *Shrek* (2001), *Vanilla Sky* (2001), *Gangs of New York* (2002), *Shrek 2* (2004), *Shrek the Third*

(2007), *Shrek Forever After* (2010), *Knight and Day* (2010), *Green Hornet* (2011), and *Bad Teacher* (2011) (Christine 2011).

In between movie roles, Cameron Diaz volunteers her time at a number of charities, events, and special causes. She took part in the *America: A Tribute to Heroes* charity telethon for victims of the September 11, 2001, terrorist attacks and participated at *Live Earth* in New York on July 7, 2007, by introducing music acts such as Bon Jovi and The Police. Here are a few of the other charities, events, and causes that Diaz has been involved with (http://www.looktothestars.org/celebrity/32-cameron-diaz):

- 4Real Foundation
- Act Green
- Centre for Environmental Education
- Declare Yourself
- Environmental Media Association
- Food Bank for New York City
- Green Tasks
- Make Poverty History
- ONE Campaign
- Racing for Kids
- Red Cross
- The Lunchbox Fund
- Unite for Japan
- Pangea Day

Perhaps the one organization that Diaz has been most recognized for and connected with is Pangea Day. As a member of its advisory board, Cameron Diaz has supported this organization because it is dedicated to creating a worldwide network of concerned citizens making a difference and believing that film can change the world.

Pangea Day started on May 10, 2008, in places such as Cairo, Kigali, London, Los Angeles, Mumbai, and Rio de Janeiro, where participants were linked for a live program of powerful films, live music, and visionary speakers. Using the Internet, television, and mobile phones, the event was broadcasted in seven languages to millions of people. Throughout the day, audiences heard from renowned entertainers, political leaders, public speakers, scholars, musicians, actors, and actresses. Diaz contributed the following message during the broadcast:

How can films change the world? They can't but the people who watch them can. By changing minds, we change the world. (http://www.pangeaday.org/aboutPangeatDay.php)

Diaz continues to donate her extra time to worthy causes, events, and charities that mean a lot to her and her personal history.

Rosario Dawson

I first saw actress Rosario Dawson in one of my favorite comedic actor Eddie Murphy's films, *The Adventures of Pluto Nash*, in 2002. Dawson played Murphy's love interest in this low-budget futuristic film, which did not perform well at the box office, but continues to do exceptionally well on cable channels year after year. By the end of the movie, Dawson had become the star of the movie—and movie audiences became more intrigued about this new actress. During that same year, she also starred in *Ash Wednesday, Men in Black II*, and Spike Lee's *25th Hour*.

An actress, writer, and singer, Rosario Dawson is of Puerto Rican, Afro-Cuban, Irish, and Native American descent. She has played a wide array of ethnicities on screen. Her movie credits include *Kids* (1995), *He Got Game* (1998), *Side Street* (1998), *Light It Up* (1999), *Down to You* (2000), *Josie and the Pussycats* (2001), *Sidewalks of New York* (2001), *Trigger Happy* (2001), *The First $20 Million Is Always the Hardest* (2002), *The Rundown* (2003; also starring Dwayne Johnson), *V-Day: Until the Violence Stops* (2003), *Alexander* (2004), *This Revolution* (2004), *Rent* (2005), *Sin City* (2005), *Clerks II* (2006), *Descent* (2007), *Eagle Eye* (2008), *Seven Pounds* (2008), *The People Speak* (2009), *SpongeBob's Truth or Square* (2009), *Percy Jackson and the Olympians: The Lightning Thief* (2010), *Unstoppable* (2010), and *Zookeeper* (2011).

Another interesting note regarding Dawson's acting career and accomplishments is that due to her multiracial identity, she has earned awards and nominations from Hispanic/Latino organizations as well as African American organizations. Her most distinguished acting awards include the American Latino Media Arts Award and the National Association of Colored People's Image award. Dawson was nominated for the 2006 ALMA Award for Outstanding Supporting Actress in the movie *Rent* and was recipient of the Image Award for Outstanding Actress for her work in the movie *Seven Pounds* (2009).

Besides receiving acting recognition for her movie performances, Dawson is a well-known activist, in and out of Hollywood. She has contributed her time to host the 10th Anniversary Benefit for the Lower East Side Girls

Club, took part in the Stay Close campaign for parents, families, and friends of lesbians and gays, and hosted a concert event in support of Global Darfur Awareness Day. Here are a few of the other charities, events, and causes that Dawson has been involved with (http://www.looktothestars.org/celebrity/500-rosario-dawson):

- Amnesty International
- Artists for Peace and Justice
- Declare Yourself
- Global Cool
- International Rescue Committee
- Make-a-Wish Foundation
- ONE Campaign
- Oxfam
- Peace Over Violence
- V-Day
- Voto Latino

Voto Latino is an organization that Dawson founded in 2004. It brings thousands of young Latinos into the political process by informing them of the local and national issues that affect their community. A nonpartisan, nonprofit, civic engagement organization, Voto Latino has produced award-winning, multimedia campaigns headlined by celebrity voices that encourage young Latinos to register to vote and get engaged in the political process in their communities. Voto Latino supporters strongly believe that it is the new generation of young American Latinos who will shape U.S. democracy in the future (http://www.votolatino.org/about).

One of the most recent issues that Voto Latino has highlighted is immigration, including the means by which President Barack Obama's administration has chosen to address it. On the group's website on May 31, 2011, the topic essay was entitled "What President Obama Can and Cannot Do on Immigration." The article provided a brief summary of the immigration issue, and then concluded with a suggestion to President Obama.

Dawson is an actress committed to raising awareness on a number of sociocultural and political issues affecting all communities, and particularly the communities with which she is most connected. Her acting career continues to grow, and her activism continues to make an impact on the social and political landscapes.

MUSIC CELEBRITIES

Music is one art form that touches almost everyone in some way or another. Whether it is music of the past, the present, or even the future, music and the music industry will always have loyal listeners and followers. With so many music styles, genres, and artists in the world today, music and those who write, produce, and sing the songs have enormous power to influence masses through their work.

Currently, two multiracial musical artists have generated millions of dollars for the music industry throughout their challenging careers: Alicia Keys and Mariah Carey.

Alicia Keys

Stunning in her looks, Alicia Keys (actual name: Alicia Augello Cook) hit the world with her debut album entitled *Songs in A Minor*, in 2001, which ultimately sold more than 12 million copies. When I first saw Alicia Keys on TV, she wore long braids and sat at the piano singing her award-winning song "Fallin." That year (2001), she became the best-selling new artist and best-selling R&B artist. Her album earned Keys five Grammy Awards in 2002, including Best New Artist and Song of the Year for "Fallin."

Keys' second studio album, *The Diary of Alicia Keys*, was released in 2003 and was another success worldwide, selling at least 8 million copies. This album also won her Grammy awards—an additional four—and was a hit on *Billboard* and R&B charts for weeks. Over the next few years, Keys continued to break new ground by doing an *MTV Unplugged* series in July 2005, releasing a third studio album in 2007 (*As I Am*), and then shifting her skills to acting for a few years and in 2013 going on a world concert tour "Set the World on Fire Tour" promoting her latest album *Girl on Fire!*.

Keys' mother is of Italian, Scottish, and Irish descent, and her father is African American. Her personal heritage and experiences may have spurred her involvement with multiple charities, events, and causes with which she has been connected over the years. Here are a few of those (http://www.looktothestars.org/celebrity/409-alicia-keys):

- DoSomething.org
- Fresh Air Fund
- 46664

- Frum Tha Ground Up
- Keep a Child Alive
- LiFEbeat
- Live 8
- Live Earth
- Nelson Mandela Foundation
- New York Coalition for Healthy School Food
- Oxfam
- Population Services International
- Raising Malawi
- (RED)
- Rush Philanthropic Arts Foundation
- Shriners Hospitals for Children
- Stand Up to Cancer
- UNICEF
- Wellness in The Schools
- YouthAIDS
- Youth Lifeline America

Keys is also the ambassador for Keep a Child Alive and has traveled to countries including Uganda, Kenya, and South Africa. She is also spokesperson for Frum Tha Ground Up, a charity dedicated to inspiring and motivating American youths to achieve success on all levels.

Her greatest impact has probably come from her work for AIDS organizations. Keys told guests at the 16th International AIDS Conference in Toronto in 2006:

We must never give up until AIDS treatment and realistic prevention messages go hand in hand across the world, until we realize that keeping mothers alive is critical to the well-being of the world's children; and until we can stand together and say, "We did not sit idly by and watch an entire continent perish." (http://www.looktothestars.org/celebrity/400-alicia-keys)

Mariah Carey

One of the most charismatic divas of our time, and one who continues to stay at the top of the charts no matter when she releases a record, is Mariah Carey. She has become an international superstar.

Carey made her recording debut in 1990 under the guidance of Columbia Records and became the first recording artist to have her first five singles top the U.S. *Billboard* Hot 100 chart. A few years later, she severed her ties with Columbia Records. Carey then reinvented herself and returned to the top of pop music in 2005 with her album *The Emancipation of Mimi*.

When asked about her background, Carey talks about her mixed heritage. Her mother is Irish American, and her father is of Afro-Venezuelan and African American descent.

Carey is another performer who feels very committed to help others. Here are some of her major charity interests and causes (http://www .looktothestars.org/celebrity/598-mariah-carey):

- American Foundation for AIDS Research
- BID 2 BEAT AIDS
- Clothes Off Our Back
- Elevate Hope Foundation
- Elton John AIDS Foundation
- Feeding America
- Fresh Air Fund
- Grammy Foundation
- Hale House Center
- Live 8
- MusiCares
- Music Rising
- Operation Smile
- Red Cross
- Save the Music Foundation
- T. J. Martell Foundation
- United Negro College Fund
- United Service Organization
- World Hunger Relief

Mariah Carey is a Congressional Horizon Award recipient for her humanitarian work and is well known for her efforts to help disadvantaged children. She is cofounder of Camp Mariah, where inner-city youth have the opportunity to embrace the arts and learn about career opportunities. She established the camp in conjunction with the Fresh Air Fund, which provides free summer vacations to children growing up in New York City's toughest neighborhoods.

SPORTS AND NEWS CELEBRITIES

In the sports and news fields, there are many multiracial individuals who have made an impact, and who are currently making an impact. In the sports field, three such individuals have consistently captured the world's attention on and off the field: Derek Jeter (New York Yankees shortstop), Hines Ward (retired Pittsburgh Steelers wide receiver), and Tiger Woods (golfer).

Derek Jeter

Derek Jeter is a future Major League Baseball "Hall of Famer" and captain of the New York Yankees, who have won multiple championships under his leadership. The premier role model as an American baseball player, his heritage includes a father of African American descent and a mother of Irish/German descent.

During Jeter's rookie year in 1996, he started the Turn 2 Foundation to promote healthy lifestyles among youth. While having dinner with his father in a Detroit hotel, Jeter decided to start his own foundation. At that moment, they laid the plans for Turn 2 (http://derekjeter.mlb.com).

The name "Turn 2" is symbolic of the double play made by infielders during a game; it also represents Jeter's uniform number—2. His foundation encourages young people to avoid drugs and alcohol (http://derekjeter.mlb.com). The program targets youths in west Michigan; Tampa, Florida; and New York City. Since its beginnings in December 1996, the Turn 2 Foundation has awarded more than $12 million in grants to promote healthy lifestyles for thousands of youth (http://derekjeter.mlb.com).

Hines Ward

Hines Ward was a National Football League All-Pro, Future Hall of Fame wide receiver for the Pittsburgh Steelers. In 2006, Ward became the first Korean American to win the Super Bowl Most Valuable Player award. Recently, he earned another title—winner of ABC's *Dancing with the Stars* competition in spring 2011.

Ward's heritage includes a father of African American descent and a mother of Korean heritage. Hines Ward was born in Seoul, Korea, before the family moved to Atlanta and East Point, Georgia.

In 2006, while visiting his birthplace of Seoul, Korea, Ward donated $1 million to create the Hines Ward Helping Hands Foundation. His foundation focuses on improving literacy among children. His foundation also provides children with programs and services to better equip them for achieving success. In Korea, the Helping Hands Foundation has targeted biracial and mixed-race children like Ward, and assists them in overcoming the discrimination often targeted at such individuals. Some of the planned fundraising activities included a celebrity fashion show featuring biracial models, a football camp to raise money for education, and a speaking tour across Korea (www.hinesward.com/helping-hands-foundation.php).

Tiger Woods

Eldrick "Tiger" Woods is an American professional golfer whose achievements to date rank him among the most successful golfers of all time. In 2006, Woods was the highest-paid professional athlete in the world, having earned an estimated $100 million from winnings and endorsements. At the end of the 2007 season, Tiger Woods was on top of the golf world again, winning the PGA Championship (http://sports.espn.go/com/golf/pgachampionship07/news/story?id=2971556).

Although his star power has dimmed in recent years due to well-publicized marital issues related to infidelity, Woods remains a unique professional athlete in the world of sports. His father was of mixed African American, Chinese, and Native American descent; his mother is of mixed Thai, Chinese, and Dutch descent. In fact, Woods refers to himself as "Cablinasian"—a term coined from the combination of Caucasian, black, (American) Indian, and Asian. Tiger's charity work primarily involves his foundation—the Tiger Woods Foundation—which seeks to help children educationally worldwide (http://web.tigerwoodsfoundation.org).

Soledad O'Brien and Ann Curry

In the news industry, there are two multiracial individuals who have been consistently successful over the years: Soledad O'Brien and Ann Curry.

CNN host and anchor Soledad O'Brien has been highly visible and groundbreaking in her documentaries (*Latino in America* and *Black in America*) and reporting. Her father is an Australian of Irish descent, and her mother is Afro-Cuban.

The former co-anchor of the NBC's *Today* morning show and an investigative journalist reporter for the network, Ann Curry has a multiracial heritage. Her father is of French, Irish, and Dutch descent, and her mother is Japanese.

Both Curry and O'Brien have been recognized by their professional organizations for their exceptional reporting, their career accomplishments, and as pioneering role models as women of color in the television news industry. Ann Curry and Soledad O'Brien are two individuals who have acknowledged their multiracial heritage to the television and print worlds without reservation.

POLITICAL FIGURES

Barack Obama

A single individual best represents multiracials today in the world of politics—U.S. President Barack Obama. Obama, the nation's 44th president and first non-Caucasian top leader, has as his heritage a Kenyan father and a Caucasian mother of Irish descent. Yet even before he became president, Obama was not a typical politician.

According to political reporter Benjamin Wallace-Wells (2004), Americans perceived Obama to be a new type of political character. He was black, but not quite. He spoke "white," with the hand gestures of a management consultant, but also demonstrated the oratorical flourishes of a black preacher. Supporters and critics have likened Obama's popular image to a cultural Rorschach test, a neutral persona on whom people can project their personal histories and aspirations. As chronicled in his best-selling books, *Dreams from My Father: A Story of Race and Inheritance* and *The Audacity of Hope: Thoughts on Reclaiming the American Dream*, Obama's own stories about his family's origins reinforce his "everyman" persona. Eugene Robinson (2007), a *Washington Post* opinion columnist, has characterized Obama's political image as follows: "the personification of both—and, a messenger who rejects 'either-or' political choices, and [one who] could move the nation beyond the cultural wars of the 1960s."

Although time will tell whether Obama moves the nation beyond the cultural wars of the 1960s, he is, of course, in a distinctly unique position not only to confront the issues facing multiracials today but, more importantly, to bring their specific issues to the forefront like no other movie, sports, or television news celebrity can.

On May 23, 2011, Obama publicly acknowledged his multiracial heritage to the world, when he visited Dublin, Ireland. Apparently, genealogists have traced his mother's roots back to Ireland and to a small town where a young shoemaker named Falmouth Kearney, Obama's great-great-great grandfather, lived during his early life. In his speech to the Irish crowd, Obama said of his great-great-great grandfather:

He left during the Great Hunger, as so many Irish did, to seek a new life in the New World. He traveled by ship to New York, where he entered himself into the records as a laborer. He married an American girl from Ohio. They settled in the Midwest. They started a family. (http://blogs.abcnews.com/politicalpunch, abstracted May 23, 2011)

So there was President Obama, in Ireland, announcing to the world his Irish ancestry. The Irish crowd praised and welcomed his acknowledgment (ABC News 2011).

Even with all the global attention and admiration for his Irish ancestry on this very political trip, however, President Obama still does not officially recognize his multiracial heritage. During the 2010 U.S. Census collection, in which every adult in the United States—including the U.S. president—completed a census report, Obama filled out his report and did not identify himself as multiracial. After media inquiries, the White House confirmed that Obama checked only the racial box that said "Black, African American, or Negro." Obama could have checked more than one racial box, or "some other race," or written in "multiracial" or even checked "white." Instead, according to media reports, Obama's 2010 census was completed as follows:

Obama filled out the form on Monday, supplying information for himself, first lady Michelle Obama and their daughters Malia and Sasha, as well as for Mrs. Obama's mother, Marian Robinson, who lives with the family in the White House. (http://www.theroot.com/print/40401, abstracted June 14, 2011)

Thus, with one stroke of the pen, President Obama set the postracial dream back incredibly. He is "officially" African American—not multiracial.

Many individuals, organizations, and activists in multiracial communities across America were surprised by, and disappointed in, the president's decision (Pittswiley 2011). For example, Michelle Hughes, president of the Chicago Biracial Family Network, said that she received several emails from surprised friends within moments of Obama's decision being made public. She explains their reaction:

> I think everybody is entitled to self-identify. If he chooses to self-identify as African American, that's his right. That being said, I think that the multiracial community feels a sense of disappointment that he refuses to identify with us. (http://articles.latimes.co/print/2010/apr/04/nation/la-na-obama-census4-2010apr04)

Yet with all the reaction from numerous multiracial community activists groups, perhaps the strongest reaction came from Private Eric Jaskolski whose letter was posted on the Internet as "A Letter to Our 'Mixed' President." Here is one excerpt from his letter to President Obama (http://nomorerace.wordpress.com/2010/01/02/a-letter-to-our-mixed-president):

> Like you President Obama, I am the blending of two races. My mother is black and my father is white. As with your mother and father, my parents were able to see and experience a love that bridged racial divides. Throughout the years, as I got older and like you, I faced some extremely difficult and joyful times . . . President Obama we cannot go back to the one-drop black blood rule . . .
>   Respectively
>   Pvt. Eric C. Jaskolski, U.S. Army

In the end, this letter sums up so much. It is up to our leaders to recognize and support multiracials, and all of their issues. We wait, now in 2013, to see if President Obama becomes supportive.

CONCLUSION

Today, all types of multiracial celebrities (movie, sports, news, and political) are leading the world to take action on a wide array of social, cultural, health, ethnic, racial, religious, educational, sports, gender, age, global, environmental, familial, and political issues. Many have been very effective in not only raising awareness of a particular issue, but also developing programs that have changed people's lives for the better. They are doing their part to change the perspective in America as it relates to issues that affect multiracials.

It is obvious that one of the key factors for changing perspectives on issues related to multiracials is to first acknowledge that you are multiracial. This is an individual decision and individual right. No one is contesting that.

Nonetheless, we realize in our society today that all of us have the ability to change the world's perspective on an issue. It really takes just one person who strongly believes in who he or she is, and is willing to take a stand for an issue or cause when others have not and will not, to make a difference. In the past, multiracials have been forced to stay silent because of society's social, cultural, political, discriminatory, and racist views and actions against them.

But we are at the start of a new day in history. It is a day in which one can feel proud to be counted as a person of mixed heritage in these United States. We no longer have to abide by the one-drop rule, which has essentially imprisoned the thinking and actions of millions across generations. It's time to stand up to be counted as multiracial in America.

ELEVEN

Global Multiracial Issues

INTRODUCTION

Sometimes, Americans believe that our societal and racial issues are unique to us. This might have been somewhat true in ways and years past, but we live in a very globalized, interconnected world today. It does not matter whether your country is a highly industrialized, technologically abundant country or a nonindustrialized country with very limited technological resources—our world is more global than ever before.

Because we are so interconnected now, we can see a basic truth that might not have been so clear before: humans are alike no matter what their individual backgrounds, circumstances, or home place on Earth. We all tend to go through the same things.

Thus it should come as no surprise that other countries around the world have faced, and developed their particular way of addressing, multiracial and mixed race issues. Like the United States, those nations have implemented discriminatory practices against those who were designated as "mixed race." From one country to another, there were—and still are—varying discriminatory practices adhered to by a majority of the population within that country.

GLOBAL OVERVIEW OF MIXED RACES

It is very difficult to approach the issue of mixed races from a global perspective, simply because many countries are not willing to document or discuss this topic in great detail. The major reason for this reluctance is that historically, mixed races were the result of one invading population or country attempting to colonize the indigenous population of another country. An example that most Americans can relate to is the history and the peopling of the United States.

When the early Europeans (English, Spanish, and French) came to settle and develop colonies in what we now refer to as the United States, they created the first mixed-race populations of Native American, African, English, Spanish, French, South American, and Caribbean heritages. The 13 English colonies that would become the original U.S. states were founded along the east coast of the New World beginning in 1607. The population of these colonies grew rapidly, from approximately 50,000 in 1650 to some 2.5 million by 1775. High birth rates and low death rates were augmented by steady flows of immigrants from Europe and slaves from the West Indies. By 1860, there were 4 million slaves residing in the United States, nearly eight times as many as had lived there in 1790 (Baird-Olson 2003). The origins and growth of the multiracial populations in the United States can be documented and used as an example of the colonization process that often happens when one country invades another (Ikeda 2007).

To condense the global overview of mixed races presented here, this section highlights specific information from a variety of online resources, but especially the superb website and blog called "Mixed in Different Shades" (http://mixedindifferentshades.net), which has organized all of this information in a user-friendly approach. This website, the blog, and the subsequent book and video documentary explore the experiences of mixed-heritage/mixed-race persons and communities throughout history across the planet. Specifically, the Mixed in Different Shades website states on its home page:

> The project does not aim to make mixed heritage people out to be better or superior to any other peoples; as we should well know—superiority or inferiority are [sic] but a state of mind. Inter-racial relationships prove that we can love each other and mixed heritage people are the living proof that human kind is one species and that underneath the white, black, yellow, red and brown skin, we are basically all the same and basically all individually different, truly mixed in different shades. (http://mixedindifferentshades.net, abstracted June 17, 2011)

EUROPE

Recently, figures released by the Official for National Statistics (ONS) of Great Britain revealed that the non-white British population of England

and Wales grew from 6.6 million in 2001 to 9.1 million in 2009—non-whites now account for nearly one in six members of this population (Rogers 2011). The data also show that there are now almost 1 million mixed-race people in the two countries.

Notably, the white British population has stayed the same since 2001. There has been an increase in births in this group, but there has also been a similar number of such people emigrating to Britain. As for the "other" white population, it has increased significantly. Specifically, an increase from 1.4 million to 1.9 million of "other" white population was not simply due to eastern Europeans arriving in Britain, but also reflected the arrival of people from Commonwealth countries such as Australia and New Zealand (Rogers 2011).

The 2011 report revealed that the non-white British population has grown by 4.1 percent per year, adding up to 37.4 percent growth—2.5 million people—over the entire period. The only group to shrink in numbers is the white Irish population—down from 646,600 in 2001 to 574,000 in 2009 due to falling birth rates and increased emigration.

The mixed-race population in England and Wales grew nearly 50 percent over the study period to reach almost 1 million for the first time—it increased from 672,000 in 2001 to 986,600 in 2009. One-third of these people are mixed African Caribbean and white, followed by Asian and white individuals. Interestingly, the ONS stated that this growth was not a result of increasing birth rates but rather occurred because "the population is mixing up more."

In north London, Haringey has the highest multiracial proportion of the total population, estimated at 4.5 percent. In north London, Brent is the most ethnically diverse borough. Slightly more than one-third of its population is considered white British, with large mixed-race, Asian, black, and Irish communities making up the rest. As a result, Brent is a vibrant place to live and work (Rogers 2011).

AFRICA

It is difficult to discuss Africa without splitting the continent into two—Arab northern Africa, which usually is regarded as part of the Arab world owing to the influence of the Ottoman Empire and the Islamic religion, and sub-Saharan Africa (Daniel 2003). For the sake of this discussion, I will highlight southern Africa.

In sub-Saharan Africa—South Africa, in particular—probably the first of the identifiable mixed-heritage communities started in the Cape of Good Hope. These people were originally known as Bastaards or Basters.

Because the British found this term offensive, their names were later changed to Griqua, due to their relatedness to the Chariguriqua, a Cape native Khoikhoi group. The Griqua/Basters are regarded as a subcategory of the more general southern African mixed race "Coloured" community (Daniel 2003).

During the apartheid era (1948–1994), to keep divisions between sub-populations and maintain a race-focused society, the government used the term "Coloured" to describe one of the four main racial groups:

1. The black Africans, which consists of several groups account for 90 percent of the black population. The black population makes up 75 percent of South Africa's entire population.
2. The whites, who account for about 13 percent of the South African population.
3. The Indians, who account for approximately 3 percent of the population.
4. The Coloureds, who are of mixed white and black descent and account for 9 percent of the population.

The black population consists of several groups: Khoi-San, Xhosa, Zulu, Ndebele, Sotho, Shangaan, and Venda. The biggest groups are Zulus (21%), Xhosas (17%), and the Sotho (15%). The Khoi-San are originally hunter-gatherers who have inhabited the land for a very long time.

As for the people categorized as Coloured, they actually originate from Dutch sailors who intermarried with the Khoi-San in the 17th century. Others are descendants of the first Dutch settlers and the native people of the Cape (Khoikhoi) or the Malays, who were taken to South Africa as slaves from East India in the 18th century. Coloured people constitute a majority of the population in Western Cape and Northern Cape provinces. Most speak Afrikaans, but approximately 10 percent of Coloureds speak English as their mother tongue, mostly in the Eastern Cape and Natal. In contrast, virtually all Cape Town Coloureds are bilingual. Some can comfortably code-switch between "Kaapse taal" (a creolized dialect of Afrikaans spoken mostly in the Cape Flats), "suiwer Afrikaans" (formal Afrikaans as taught at school), and English (Daniel 2003).

ASIA

In general, Asia consists of three very large major regions: North Asia (China, Japan, North Korea, South Korea, and Mongolia), South Asia

(India, Sri Lanka, Afghanistan, Bangladesh, Bhutan, Maldives, Nepal, and Pakistan), and South East Asia (Indonesia, Burma, Cambodia, East Timor, Laos, Malaysia, Myanmar, Philippines, Singapore, Thailand, and Vietnam). Contact and mixture between Asian and Indo-European peoples has a long history, dating back several thousands of years to the spread of the Indo-Europeans into Central and Northern Asia.

The word "Eurasian" refers to people of mixed Asian and European ancestry. Many Eurasian ethnic groups arose during the Mongol invasion of Europe and the colonial occupation of Asian regions by European states and private corporations that started with the great wave of European naval expansion and exploration in the 16th century and continues to the present. The main European colonial powers were Spain and Portugal in the 16th century, followed by the Netherlands, the United Kingdom, and France from the 17th century onward.

For example, between 1602 and 1796, the Dutch East India Company sent almost 1 million Europeans—not all Dutch—to work in Asia. These immigrants settled mainly in the Dutch East Indies, which eventually expanded to become Indonesia. Indonesia is a country in Southeast Asia and Oceania. It is a chain of 17,000 islands stretching almost 4,000 kilometers from east to west. Indonesia is home to approximately 300 ethnic groups, each with its own cultural identity and its own history, whose heritage was influenced by peoples of Indian, Arabic, Chinese, and European descent. Therefore, there are a number of mixed races identified in this region of Southeast Asia.

Examples of mixed-race populations in the Southeast Asia region include the Vietnamese Eurasians and Amerasians. After the First Indochina War and under the terms of the Geneva Accords of 1954, many of the French troops took thousands of Vietnamese wives and children home with them, while approximately 100,000 Eurasians stayed in Vietnam (Nimmons 2011). In a deal negotiated by both countries, France offered Vietnamese Eurasians the opportunity of citizenship and an education at the age of 18. Many Vietnamese Eurasian youths took advantage of this opportunity, and later arranged for their mothers to join them in France.

The Amerasians, in contrast, were the offspring of American soldiers and Vietnamese women during and after the Vietnam War (1955–1975). In 1975, after the withdrawal of U.S. troops from Vietnam, approximately 30,000 Amerasian children were left fatherless in a culture where the father is the symbol of the household. Because of this status, they were looked down upon among their own people. Those who were fortunate to immigrate to the United States also struggled because the United States did not recognize the children of the U.S. soldiers born in Vietnam as U.S. citizens; thus these children were somewhat forgotten as well (Nimmons 2011).

In northern Asia—Japan, for example—persons who are identified as mixed race are referred to as "Hafu," meaning somebody who is half-Japanese. The word "Hafu" comes from the English word "half," indicating half-foreignness. This label emerged in the 1970s in Japan and is now the most commonly used label and preferred term of self-definition for multiracials in that country. Interestingly, in modern Japan, the Hafu image is projected as an ideal type: English ability, international cultural experience, and Western physical features—tall with long legs, small head and face, yet often looking Japanese enough for the majority to feel comfortable with (King and DeCosta 1996; Hafu Japanese.org 2010).

According to Japanese governmental statistics, there were only 5,545 recorded interracial marriages in that country in 1980. By 2001, this trend reached its peak, with 39,727 interracial marriages being recorded—seven times the 1980 figure. A large number of these interracial marriages were between Japanese and Chinese persons, followed by Japanese and Filipinos, and Japanese and Korean individuals. Other interracial marriages included American-Japanese, Brazilian-Japanese, and British-Japanese unions. Overall, the Hafu population is growing dramatically in Japan.

SOUTH AND CENTRAL AMERICA

The story of the lower Americas, and particularly Latin America, is a story of Spanish colonialism. Although Spain and Portugal eventually claimed most of Latin America and the Caribbean in the late 1500s, they were not without serious rivals. Other European states—England, France, and Holland—also competed with Spain and Portugal for dominion over the New World, especially over the Caribbean islands and the northern coastlines of Central and South America (Sanabria 2007: 77). This ongoing competition in colonizing parts of this region resulted in a complex linguistic, political, historical, religious, cultural, and racial groupings (Sanabria 2007).

In the early colonial period, pseudoracial categories including *mestizo* (a highly complex and fluid intermediary category between Indian and white; *mestico*, Portuguese) and mulatto (a similarly complex category between black and white) were created, among many others, and served as intermediate categories between white and black or Indian, seen to be located at the polar extremes of the emerging racial classification system. According to Sanabria (2007), in the early colonial period, these intermediate categories were recognized as being the result of mixed biological ancestry. For example, a *mestizo* (*mestiza* for a female) was a child born to Indian and Spanish or Portuguese parents. Typically, the father was Spanish or Portuguese and the mother was Indian, reflecting the demographics of the early colonial period, when there were far fewer European women in the Americas.

As unions between Spanish or Portuguese men and Indian or African women produced large numbers of children of mixed ancestry, the categories of *mestizo* and mulatto, respectively, came to reflect the emerging racial diversity. Sanabria (2007) notes that over time, racial classification became increasingly complex, as generations of mixing led to multiple intermediate categories in places such as Mexico, Cuba, and Brazil; in general, it became more difficult to readily distinguish members of different categories based on physical appearance alone. In Brazil, for example, scholars found more than 40 different racial terms used in the community to distinguish members of various types of mixed ancestry.

In 2010, a census survey indicated that Brazil had become for the first time a "majority minority" nation, meaning that less than half the population now identifies as white (Barnes 2011). Every minority racial group—officially, "black," "pardo" (mixed), "yellow," and "indigenous"—has grown in absolute numbers since 2000. "White" was the only group that shrank in both absolute numbers and percentage over this period, with its share falling from 53 percent of the total population 10 years ago to 48 percent today. Specifically, people who declared themselves black on the 2010 census numbered approximately 14.5 million, representing 7.6 percent of Brazil's 190 million total population, while the pardo population (mixed and loosely translated as "brown") grew to 82.3 million, or 43.1 percent of the total population.

Researchers suspect that this shift reflects not only an increase in biracial unions that produced mixed-race children, but also a growing comfort with not calling oneself white as a prerequisite to prospering in Brazil, a trend that underscores the growing influence of popular culture. Professor Mirando-Rieiro commented on this new shift: "People who might have hidden this side [of their race] in the past now see it's an advantage" (Barnes 2011).

Finally, the increased numbers of individuals preferring to identify themselves as black and mixed race are a result of the growth of Brazil's middle class, a trend that is increasing the wealth of the country's black and mixed-race populations. Brazilian scholar Fundacao Getulio Vargars says that about half of blacks and mixed raced people now belong to the middle class (Barnes 2011).

CONCLUSION

This brief overview of the world's mixed-race populations reveals that every part of our world, from the very beginning of each civilization,

TWELVE

Multiracials: Speaking Out about the Issues

INTRODUCTION

This book's themes included attention to two primary factors that have caused a dramatic increase in the number of multiracials in the United States:

1. An increase in interracial relationships and marriages
2. The new cultural trend of recognizing and accepting one's multiracial and multiethnic heritage

It has taken the U.S. Census and the federal government decades to allow individuals to state that they are of two or more races. This acknowledgment is a major positive cultural shift in American society.

Although it has been a major struggle for many multiracials to find and establish themselves in society, both locally and nationally, they have continuously challenged the cultural rules governing race relations in America. The "one-drop" rule is a prime example of a cultural rule that both historically and currently discriminates against and divides all those who adhere to its implementation.

Yet the major issues associated with multiracials are not just about race. Instead, these issues involve their biology, health, and lifestyle. This book highlighted many significant biological, health, and lifestyle topics that scholars have largely neglected to study, such as multiracial physical features, health disparities among multiracial groups, bone marrow transplant difficulties, and transracial adoption issues.

The accomplishments of multiracial celebrities in the United States and understanding of how the rest of the world interacts with their multiracial populations provide us with significant evidence that our world has accepted and embraced multiracials. They also indicate how multiracials are changing, and might change, our world.

To assure that this book offers teachable moments, and that the reader clearly understands how multiracials feel about issues that have affected their lives in the past and today, this chapter presents personal and cultural comments to questions that I posed to multiracial people, in a semi-structured, open-ended questionnaire.

MULTIRACIALS SPEAK OUT

For the 10 questions posed to them, here are some of the responses from participants, whom I choose to call "informants."

1. **In the United States, every individual is asked to identify himself or herself with a particular race and/or ethnic group. How do you identify yourself?**

   Informant #2: *Multiracial.*

   Informant #3: *Identify my race as black and white and my ethnicity as Latino.*

   Informant #4: *For years, I identified myself as black only, because my mother was black, and all of the relatives I knew and were around were black as well. Today, I have started to include the other ethnicities I am mixed with when identifying myself.*

   Informant #5: *I identify myself as a biracial American. My mother is African American and my father was German American. I will say that I tend to identify more with African American because my mother raised us without my father.*

   Informant #6: *I identify myself as Hawaiian, Portuguese, Puerto Rican, and African American.*

2. **What do you think of the U.S. Census category of multiracial people? Approve or disapprove? View link: http://www .censusscope.org/us/chart_multi.html.**

   Informant #1: *I am conflicted. On the one hand, I do agree with the need to identify/collect data on residents' ethnicity so that the government can measure diversity. On the other hand, I find it more ideal if all of us could be identified as "Americans" because to me it would symbolize a color-blind society. However, I am discovering that it is important to recognize and emphasize ethnicity and race so that it is well understood that this country is not a homogenous society.*

Informant #2: *I approve, as long as we are actually counted as multiracial.*

Informant #3: *I approve of it because it allows persons to check exactly what they identify themselves with. It does not take away from a specific group and it leaves very little room for debate.*

Informant #4: *I agree. It is long overdue.*

Informant #5: *I'm assuming Hispanic is consumed as part of the other category, which I think is a mistake considering the growth of the Hispanic population in the U.S. . . . But, then again I don't know that "Hispanic" is considered a race or an ethnicity. Since Hispanic is not included, that leads me to believe that the Census probably considers Hispanic an ethnicity and not a race. Overall, I disapprove because I think the data need to be more concise to include Hispanics—maybe a multi-ethnicity distribution profile instead?*

Informant #6: *I think the U.S. Census created a vague description of multiracial people. Many individuals have different concepts of race, which in return can create a confusing questionnaire. I often experience this confusion when filling out applications. The census may allow individuals to select more than one race, but individuals still feel restrained in how many they can select. It also is an example of the many combinations of races that exist in multiracial populations. I did find it interesting that Hawaii was one of the top states for multiracial populations and the most common combination was Asian and Hawaiian or Other Pacific Islander.*

3. **Does it matter to you on how you are categorized within a racial and/or ethnic category? If so, please explain.**

Informant #1: *I don't mind being categorized in a particular racial and/or ethnic category. I am proud of my heritage and if my representation means that it will contribute positively to diversity awareness in the U.S., I am more than happy being "categorized."*

Informant #2: *It does matter to me because I care about the truth.*

Informant #3: *It does not matter as long as I am being counted for each race I identify with or as a multiracial person.*

Informant #4: *It matters to me now. The variety of ethnicities I am mixed with combined together make me who I am.*

Informant #5: *It used to matter to me when I was younger growing up, especially in my early teens when I was searching to find my identity ... but now it does not matter as much personally. If someone asks me, I will self-identify my ethnicity and race but I find that it matters less and less to me as I grow older.*

Informant #6: *Yes and no. Yes, because often certain races or ethnic groups are always grouped together. For example, when asked about my race on applications I usually have to identify as Pacific Islander/Asian even though I do not consider myself Asian. Other times it does not matter because I am used to people trying to guess my racial background.*

4. **Do you think more people in the United States will identify themselves as multiracial each year? If so, why?**

Informant #2: *Yes, because if the option is there for people who fit that category, then I do believe people will identify that way. People who want to acknowledge all that encompasses who they are. Although there are some multiracial people who allow the racist one-drop rule to dictate that if there is any African descent, then they should be considered black, despite how little the amount.*

Informant #3: *I think so. There has been an increase since the 2000 census; organizations for persons of multiracial heritage are popping up on college campuses, and I feel the new generation is not as reluctant to define themselves as multiracial or biracial as those of us who are early/late Generation Xers and baby boomers.*

Informant #4: *Yes, I think this will continue to increase. More and more multiracial people are getting a voice, and are not ashamed to freely express themselves any longer. More are realizing they do not "fit" with just one racial group, and many are realizing this for the first time.*

Informant #5: *Yes, I do. I believe that racial differences are becoming more accepted in the U.S., and that the election of President Obama into office is a good example of this trend. I also think that interracial couples and families are more accepted and encouraged than ever before and that we will continue to see more "crossing over" as the country continues to diversify.*

Informant #6: *More people will identify themselves as multiracial each year because of the mixing of races and ethnic groups in the United States. In return, people are also becoming more accepting of their diverse backgrounds and identifying with more than one race.*

5. **Why do you think it has taken the United States so long to recognize multiracial groups?**

Informant #2: *I think there are several reasons. First of all, there are many more multiracial people who exist now than ever before. Secondly, even though many people of mixed heritage don't feel that they truly belong in one category or the other, those people were afraid to challenge the racist system of labeling people according to what was considered the least desirable race. I feel that today we still have a long way to go because many Americans of European descent don't want people with African ancestry polluting their race. I don't think they have a problem with multiracial people being acknowledged as multiracial, as long as we don't consider ourselves white, but many people of African descent want to include us in theirs. It seems to me that most black people feel the same about race as white people do. That black is undesirable and white is desirable. Therefore many black people want to point to multiracial people and say "look how white black people can look," which they can't do without us. I don't know why else black people want to hold on to the one-drop rule. I don't know why else they don't speak out against the racism of it. If black people were truly proud of being black, they wouldn't want us included in their race, especially those of us who are almost pure white. It seems that black people are trying to dilute their race and white people are trying to hold on to theirs.*

Informant #4: *Sadly, multiracial people mostly kept their feelings to themselves, and did not share them openly. They quietly chose one race to bond with, or identify with, often in vain, and to no avail. I think either they thought they had no choice, or [thought that way was] easier, and without controversy.*

Informant #5: *I honestly think it has been a power struggle from the start. In early U.S. history, the majority race felt the need to keep the minority race separate and beneath them in order to remain in power. I think it has been an evolving struggle or letting go of that "power" and coming to acceptance. There were probably some issues with categorizing each race, as I talked about earlier with the Hispanic dilemma.*

Informant #6: *The main issue is the stigma created by racism. Given the haunting history surrounding race in this country, it makes it difficult to recognize multiracial groups. Race is a topic often avoided and ignored.*

6. **Do you think a vast majority of Americans are aware of the major increase of multiracial populations in the next 20–30 years? If not, why?**

Informant # 2: *I think so, because more interracial couples are having children now than ever before.*

Informant #3: *I think they are aware, but choose not to discuss it in detail. There have always been multiracial people whether if they were mulattos or "mixed;" however, what I am seeing is use of the terms "biracial" or "multiracial" seems offensive to some. I noticed if I say I am black and white or mixed, then I don't get such a negative reaction. Just like there have always been gays in our society but now they want (and deserve) equal rights, particularly with marriage—and I think society is having a hard time dealing with it. They are okay with gays having "civil unions" but the word "marriage" can be controversial.*

Informant #4: *I think they are aware of it, and many of them are afraid. They feel there will be no lines to separate or divide the races any longer. Everyone will be mixed, or the same, with no difference, and that is scary to some. No one group will be superior any longer, or inferior. This is why those people work so hard to try to discourage racial mixing.*

Informant #5: *I would think so, but I am not sure. Being encapsulated in this college environment makes it difficult to be in touch with the working-class world. If people are walking around the city, and going to public places, or taking trips anywhere— I think they will be able to visually see the multiracial population increase. Unfortunately, the world is not like the college campus, so it's possible normal everyday folks are not as aware as I would like them to be.*

Informant #6: *I do not think the majority of Americans are aware of the major increase of multiracial populations. Despite our growth from racism, race is still a controversial topic. I believe people are still trained to think "white" or "black" and get*

confused by any "gray" area. They still feel compelled to catego-
rize people and the "gray" (multiracial) area creates havoc in
this categorical system.

7. **How would you describe a multiracial person? Please elaborate.**

Informant #1: *My personal description of a multiracial person is*
one that has a prominent race of color within his/her genetics.
I realize that I am placing emphasis on physical attributes, and
it is because a person of color [has historically] endured more
prejudices and adversities due to his/her appearance. However,
I do find an individual born to parents of opposite religious faiths
quite fascinating. Someone with a Jewish mother and a Catholic
father is certainly multiracial.

Informant #2: *The offspring of two or more recognized racial*
groups. That is my definition.

Informant #3: *Multiracial is not just a person who is part of two or*
more racial groups; it is about culture and how we relate to that
culture. It is also being able to identify how we see fit based on
our culture and life experiences. One of the things multiracial per-
sons who are of black descent are constantly accused of is not iden-
tifying with our black side. What these persons fail to realize is that
many of us DO in fact identify with being black, to the point where
we have only identified with being black for large portion of our
lives up until a certain point. Then we realize there is another her-
itage that we are part of that we have not explored, so it seems like
we are embracing one side more than another. However, with
being part of two or more races, it is easy to relate to one more
than the other, and that doesn't mean we are "shunning" it. Life
experiences shape us into the persons that we become, and that
includes what racial group(s) we identify with.

Informant #4: *Some of the richest, most physically beautiful people*
ever created. Being mixed with more than one ethnic group, their
background and culture [are] very diverse. They often have the
opportunity to experience these cultures on a daily basis. Fea-
tures of each race are often seen in their outward appearance,
which is stunning to see. It is very intriguing to notice how each
race is represented in the appearance of the individual person.
However, when outside, negative influences are allowed to infil-
trate their spirit, this same group of people can become tor-
mented, rejected, and confused, which is a travesty.

Informant #5: *Well, I describe myself as multiracial or biracial to be specific for people. I am clearly a product of two people of different races, so it makes sense to describe myself that way. I have found that some people don't recognize that I am biracial and assume I am some shade of either white or black—which I find pretty amusing at times. I think of a multiracial person as someone who has parents of different races, but I think it also applies to people whose parents are multiracial. But then again, how many multiracial generations does one have to trace back before the description is "diluted" out? If that were the case, then plenty of Americans are multiracial and should be aware, right? I think the problem is that people of multiracial descent who don't necessarily look like it, or feel like it, will be the hardest group to persuade. They are probably less likely to identify as multiracial if they are already comfortable identifying as only one race.*

Informant #6: *I would describe a multiracial person as someone who identifies with more than one race, which means they accept and practice the culture of each racial background. This combination of different races creates a myriad of traits and values.*

8. **Do you think other countries around the world have recognized and respected their multiracial populations as compared to the United States? Please elaborate. For example, think about the United Kingdom, Japan, and Canada.**

Informant #1: *I am wracking my brain and would like to state that there are indeed other countries that handle multiracial populations so much better than the United States. I think of Canada and the Netherlands but the percentage of these countries' multiracial population is miniscule or pales in comparison with the U.S. multiracial population. Is it thus easier to recognize multiethnics because there is no threat for this population to grow [so] rapidly that they become the majority group in 30–40 years? I feel that racism is inherent in every country, whether the issue is over race, religion, or creed. The question is how well certain countries "manage" racism.*

Because I am more familiar with how Americans view diversity and less knowledgeable about how Europeans handle such (in terms of overt examples and situations), I would presume that other countries such as Canada and the Netherlands lend more respect toward their multicultural populations.

Informant #2: *Most multiracial Spanish-speaking people are recognized as "Latino." The only difference between myself and most Latinos is that I don't speak Spanish and I'm from the United States. I don't know anything about Europe, Asia, or Canada.*

Informant #4: *The United States is a country which is obsessed with race, while other countries are not so much. I believe the other countries mentioned do have more of a respect for and appreciation of people of multiracial heritage than the U.S. The U.S. is very immature in this aspect. [Americans] want to overlook this population, or criticize them. They want to discourage the growth of it, and their independence as a group of their very own, which is ludicrous.*

Informant #6: *Yes and no. I feel that other countries are more open-minded when it comes to race, but issues surrounding race still exist. Furthermore, most countries do not have the stigmatizing history of race and racism. This makes it easier for them to respect multiracial populations.*

9. **Is there any message that you would share with others about being a multiracial person?**

Informant #1: *My childhood in Canada was significant. My first day in school in a fourth-grade classroom with a bunch of Canadians was intimidating. But my classmates were sweet and welcomed me with open arms. I was a novelty—brown, skinny, and fashioned [with] a bowl hairstyle! There weren't too many Filipinos in the mid-1970s in Ottawa, Ontario, and I didn't notice other "visible" minorities in droves. I had classmates of African, Asian, and Indian descent, but all of us combined formed perhaps a dozen minorities in our high school of approximately 300 students. It seemed then that Italians formed the largest ethnic population in the province of Ontario. It was thus important for me to have assimilated into the mainstream culture and thus be more "Canadian."*

When I was 18 years old, I moved to Dale City, California, in the San Francisco Bay area, where I was exposed to a community of Filipinos and other Asian and Hispanic groups. This was a pivotal point in my life because I reconnected with my ethnicity. Because I was surrounded by multiracial friends and family, I felt comfortable being in my own skin.

Despite the inequalities that exist today in the United States, I believe with progress, sustained efforts, and the influence of scholars and leaders who keep our hearts and minds open, this country will become intrinsically a multiracial nation.

Informant #2: *It is a matter of fact that there are multiracial people in the world. It is a matter of fact that multiracial people don't truly belong in any one category. It's time for people like us to be recognized for what we really are, and it's time that we are able to openly say, "No, I'm not black or white. I'm multiracial."*

Informant #5: *Being multiracial has allowed me to develop a unique perspective of the world. I have been able to be fully immersed in each of my ethnic cultures, yet have also been like a third party observing them. That has been the fun part. The difficult part was trying to identify as a teenager, and feeling like I didn't belong with either race. I am fortunate to be alive during a time where attitudes and ideas about race are finally changing, and folks in the U.S. are beginning to embrace diversity like never before. I think it is important that we keep the ball rolling, and continue to find self-acceptance in this developing multiracial society.*

Informant #6: *Given how people favor categorizing things, racial identity can create problems for multiracial individuals. It is difficult trying to fit into "groups" because even as a multiracial person, you still do not fit in completely. Society puts pressure [on] identifying with a specific race, and it makes it hard for multiracial people to feel accepted.*

CONCLUSION

These are the thoughts, feelings, values, opinions, and perspectives of a selected number of individuals who have identified themselves as multiracial. They, along with their family members and friends, are facing a world that is perhaps still not ready for them.

What really matters, even more so now in 2013, is that it is not about "them" or "they." It is about "us"—all of us. All of us in current "traditional" racial groupings (African Americans, Hispanic/Latinos, Asian and Pacific Islanders, Native Americans and Alaskan Natives, and Caucasians) are actually multiracial, whether we officially identify ourselves as such in the U.S. census or not. No individual or group should really consider itself a "one-drop" group, because we all have countless numbers of "drops" of blood from various racial groupings, based on our shared histories and experiences. To limit oneself to one racial group based on the one-drop rule is to denounce a diverse heritage and struggles across time. That's how we—the American people—became Americans. We were and still are a melting pot of all types of racial and ethnic groups bonded by our physical traits, language, history, religious orientation, faith and spirituality, education, occupations, values, biases, politics, income, place of birth, place of upbringing, region of the country, gender, sexual orientation, physical and mental disabilities, and—most importantly—*culture*.

As I have said in previous books and repeat here, it is our *culture* and *our shared cultural experiences* that will bring all of us truly together. May we face the future and embrace our multiracial heritages, all as members of the human race.

THIRTEEN

The Future of Our World: The Multiracial, Multiethnic Majority

INTRODUCTION

Imagine a world in which those who are the so-called minorities become the majority. In the not-too-distant future, America's "minorities" will become the majority. It is not unreasonable to conjecture that not so many decades later—by 2100—multiracials, who are now the smallest minority of the minorities and have just recently come under the government's statistical radar, will become the majority population in this nation. Most people in the country will boast a multiracial, mixed-race heritage. This is indeed our future, not just in the United States, but worldwide, with the predominant people officially identified as multiracial.

Some might argue that such thinking is more akin to science fiction. Surely, if the 1960s classic science-fiction writer, Rod Serling of the *Twilight Zone*, had written a script where most people on Earth were multiracial, the reaction from television viewers of that era probably would have sparked great controversy, with intellectuals debating the social and racial ramifications of a predominately multiracial society on all types of talk shows.

What will such a world be like?

Perhaps it will be a world where every person feels pride, vitality, and even honor to be classified as a multiracial person. A world in all of us are indeed equal because all of us are multiracial!

THE YEAR 2100

A mere 87 years from now, it will be the year 2100. That's all—just 87 years and our world will be in a new century. And what a new century it will be!

Because of the continual world population growth; the elimination of social, political, religious, cultural, and racial barriers regarding interracial dating and marriage; and especially the increasing prestige, status, and pride inherent in identifying oneself as "multiracial," all types of multiracial populations could dramatically flourish, and outnumber all types of single-race groups. Thus, in the United States, the traditional racial groupings of Caucasians, Hispanic/Latinos, Asians Americans, Native Americans and Alaskan Natives, Pacific Islanders, and African Americans could be outnumbered by multiracial groups, 2 to 1.

So what could it be like in the year 2100, with the U.S. population made up of predominantly multiracials? Will multiracials be experiencing similar issues then as they are today? What will be the general physical type associated with the majority of multiracials—and will physical appearance really matter? What will be their major health issues? Will there be any health disparity problems with the various multiracial populations? Finally, how will other "traditional" racial groups perceive their status in society compared to multiracials? These are legitimate questions to ask and to conjecture about.

Physical traits such as skin color, height, weight, hair texture, nose shape, eye shape, eye color, and overall body type will be noticeably different from these characteristics in the "traditional" racial groups in America today. For example, skin color has always been a dividing marker between the "traditional" racial groups in America. Whether one was white, brown, black, or slightly tanned, skin color was a visible marker that society used to determine the racial group to which one belonged. Although a person's skin color is actually an adaptation to (protection from) the ultraviolet rays from the sun, people in America and around the world came to believe that individuals and groups who were darker skinned were also of lesser status, less prestige, less monetary worth, and less attractiveness. This is, of course, a wrong-headed belief system.

However, by 2100, the exact opposite could become a part of the belief system and the primary pattern among a majority of Americans. That is, multiracials of color, whether of darker brown, medium brown, light brown, and darker shades of white, could be seen and treated by societal members as more prestigious, of higher status, and more attractive than other "traditional" racial groups, primarily because their numbers have dramatically increased so the physical traits associated with multiracials become the majority's preferred pattern. Multiracials will reflect *physically* the diversity of human populations around the world.

MULTIRACIAL HEALTH STATUS: 2100

Because more and more individuals of various "traditional" single-race groups will begin to re-identify themselves as multiracial, more studies seeking specific clinical and survey health data will be undertaken and their results organized in databases across the country. As researchers and health professionals analyze these health data, certain trends will become apparent.

In 2100, multiracials' life expectancy may be higher than that for the "traditional" racial groupings, because the multiracial majority will tend to be of higher income level, will demonstrate higher educational attainment, and will have better access to medical care facilities and specialists due to their places of residence and higher-status jobs. The issue of bone marrow transplants may be far less a concern for multiracials, because with an increasing population there will be more donors and potential matches.

MULTIRACIAL SOCIAL STATUS: 2100

Multiracial celebrities could dominate in the movie and television industries, sports fields, music industry, and news industry. They could also dominate district, region, state, and national political offices. The United States will likely have its first self-professed multiracial president by 2100. Certainly, throughout that presidency, major issues associated with multiracials in America will be given full recognition, support, investment, policy, and action by the federal government.

CONCLUSION

America is changing before our eyes, and we are in the midst of a dramatic population shift in which "minorities" in 2013 will definitely become the "majority" within a few decades. Demographers say the current census data provide the clearest confirmation of a changing social order, one in which racial and ethnic minorities will become the U.S. majority by midcentury. Moreover, the most interesting, most surprising developments over the coming decades may well be associated with the group that now represents the most "minority" of our minorities—multiracials.

Glossary

For those who are unfamiliar with the terms in this book, here are my definitions. These terms also have multiple meanings so there are some wide variations of their definitions depending upon one's perspective.

Afroasian: a person of African and Asian heritage.

Amerasian: a person who is racially mixed Asian. Originally referred to children of American and Asian national origin, fathered by U.S. servicemen.

Biracial: a person whose parents are of two different designated racial groups.

Eurasian: a person of Asian and white European heritage.

Hapa haole or hapa: a person of Asian or Pacific Island origin mixed with European heritage.

Hypodescent: a social, cultural, and political system that assigns a racially mixed person to the racial group that has the least social status in the society.

*Mestiza(o)***:** a person of Indian and Spanish ancestry or a person of Latino and European ancestry.

Miscegenation: race mixing in intimate dating and sexual relationships.

Monoracial: a person who claims a single racial heritage.

Mulatta(o): a person of mixed black and white ancestry.

Multiracial: a person of two or more racial heritages.

Transracial: the movement of a person across racial lines.

APPENDIX 1

Multiracial and Multiethnic Organizations and Websites

Association of Multiethnic Americans, Inc.

The Association of Multiethnic Americans is a nationwide organization representing multiracial and multiethnic communities in the United States. www.ameasite.org

Blended People of America

Blended People of America is an online community where mixed-race people learn about and discuss issues related to their community. Its website also features entertainment news that focuses on multiracial, multicultural members of the entertainment community. http://blended peopleamerica.com

MAVIN Foundation

The MAVIN Foundation publishes *MAVIN* magazine and the *Multiracial Child Resource Book* and administers the MatchMaker Bone Marrow Project. www.mavinfoundation.org

MixedFolks.com

This website is geared toward persons with multiple-race backgrounds. It provides news about famous people, message boards, and resources. www.mixedfolks.com

Multiracial Americans of Southern California (MASC)

Multiracial Americans of Southern California seeks to expand self-understanding and the general public's understanding of today's interracial, multiethnic, and cross-cultural society by facilitating interethnic dialogue and providing cultural, educational, and recreational activities. www.mascsite.org

Multiracial Organization of Students at Tufts (MOST)

The Multiracial Organization of Students at Tufts is an effort by students to create a community, forum, and an awareness of multiraciality and its associated issues, topics, and debates. The group seeks to bridge racial, ethnic, and cultural divides by creating an amalgamation of beautiful diversity. www.ase.tufts.edu/most

National Association of Mixed Student Organizations (NAMSO)

NAMSO was developed in an effort to provide a central place—that is, a national clearinghouse—of resources, information, advice, events, and networking for multiracial/multiethnic/multicultural student organizations, student leaders, and activities. www.facebook.com/mixedstudentorgs

Project RACE

Project RACE provides support and advocates for multiracial children, multiracial adults, and their families through multiracial education and community awareness. www.projectrace.com

Swirl, Inc.

This organization provides support to mixed-race families, mixed-race individuals, transracial adoptees, and interracial/cultural couples. www.swirlinc.org

APPENDIX 2

Multiracial and Multiethnic Suggested Readings

Bernstein, Mary, and Marcie De la Cruz. "What Are You? Explaining Identity as a Goal of the Multiracial Hapa Movement." *Social Problems* 56, no. 4 (2009): 722–745.

Brackett, Kimberly, Ann Marcus, Nelya McKenzie, Larry Mullins, Zongli Tang, and Annette Allen. "The Effects of Multiracial Identification on Students' Perceptions of Racism." *Social Science Journal* 43 (2006): 437–444.

Brown, Monica. "A New Multicultural Population: Creating Effective Partnerships with Multiracial Families." *Intervention in School and Clinic* 45, no. 2 (2009): 124–131.

Chideya, Farai. "How We Should Prepare for Multiracial America." *Essence* 29, no. 11 (1999): 162.

Cole, Erin, and Deborah Valentine. "Multiethnic Children Portrayed in Children's Picture Books." *Child and Adolescent Social Work Journal* 17, no. 4 (2000): 305–317.

Collins, James, and G. Reginald Daniel. "Multiracial Identity on the College Campus." *Interrace* 6, no. 3 (1995): 24.

Cruz-Janzen, Marta I. "Lives in the Crossfire: The Struggle of Multiethnic and Multiracial Latinos for Identity in a Dichotomous and Racialized World." *Race, Gender & Class* 9, no. 2 (2002): 47.

Davis, Angelique. "Multiracialism and Reparations: The Intersection of the Multiracial Category and Reparations Movements." *Thomas Jefferson Law Review* 29, no. 2 (2007): 161.

Davis, Bonnie. *The Biracial and Multiracial Student Experience: A Journey to Racial Literacy.* Thousand Oaks, CA: Corwin Press, 2009.

D'Souza, Dinesh. *The End of Racism: Principles for a Multiracial Society.* Tampa, FL: Free Press, 1995.

Edou, Tracey Lin. *One Box Is Difficult to Check: An Exploration of Parenting Multiracial and Multiethnic Children.* ProQuest Dissertations and Theses, 2010.

Flores, Glenda. *Latina Teachers in Los Angeles: Navigating Race/Ethnic and Class Boundaries in Multiracial Schools.* ProQuest Dissertations and Theses, 2011.

Gullickson, Aaron, and Ann Morning. "Choosing Race: Multiracial Ancestry and Identification." *Social Science Research* 40 (2011): 498–512.

Iceland, John. "Beyond Segregation: Multiracial and Multiethnic Neighborhoods in the United States." *Social Forces* 85, no. 3 (2005): 1444.

Jackson, Kelly. "Living the Multiracial Experience: Shifting Racial Expressions, Resisting Race, and Seeking Community." *Qualitative Social Work* 11, no. 1 (2012): 42–60.

Jackson, Kelly, and Gina Samuels. "Multiracial Competence in Social Work: Recommendations for Culturally Attuned Work with Multiracial People." *Social Work* 56, no. 3 (2011): 235.

Jayaraman, Saru, and Aarti Shahani. "Collective Prosperity: The Power of a Multiethnic Agenda: A New York Model." *Harvard Journal of Hispanic Policy* 20 (2007): 15.

Jobe, Jared, Diane O'Rourke, Richard Warnecke, Timothy Johnson, Patricia Golden, and Noel Chavez. "Dimensions of Self-Identification among Multiracial and Multiethnic Respondents in Survey Interviews." *Evaluation Review* 21, no. 6 (1997): 671–687.

Khanna, Nikki. *Biracial in America: Forming and Performing Racial Identity.* Lanham, MD: Lexington Books, 2011.

Khanna, Nikki. "The Role of Reflected Appraisals in Racial Identity: The Case of Multiracial Asians." *Social Psychology Quarterly* 67, no. 2 (2004): 115–131.

Kurashige, Scott. "Crenshaw and the Rise of Multiethnic Los Angeles." *Afro-Hispanic Review* 27, no. 1 (2008): 41.

Kwan, SanSan, and Kenneth Speirs. *Mixing It Up: Multiracial Subjects.* Austin, TX: University of Texas Press, 2004.

Lewan, Todd. "Multiracial Americans See Attitudes Evolving." *Louisiana Weekly* 82, no. 40 (2008): 1.

Luk, Chiu, Eric Fong, Chen Wenhong, and Emily Anderson. "The Logic of Ethnic Business Distribution in Multiethnic Cities: 1." *Urban Affairs Review* 43, no. 4 (2008): 497–519.

Manuel, Ramirez. *Multicultural/Multiracial Psychology: Mestizo Perspective in Personality and Mental Health.* Lanham, MD: Jason Aronson, Inc., 1998.

Masuoka, Natalie. "The Multiracial Option: Social Group Identity and Changing Patterns of Racial Categorization." *American Politics Research* 39, no. 1 (2011): 176–204.

Nazroo, James. *Health and Social Research in Multiethnic Societies.* London: Routledge, 2006.

Potter, Gina. *The Invisibility of Multiracial Students: An Emerging Majority by 2050.* ProQuest Dissertations and Theses, 2009.

Putman, John. "White, Black, and Yellow: Rethinking Multiethnic Los Angeles." *Reviews in American History* 37, no. 1 (2009): 110.

Rainer, Spencer. *Challenging Multiracial Identity.* Boulder, CO: Lynne Reiner Publishers, 2006.

Romo, Rebecca. "Between Black and Brown: Blaxican (Black-Mexican) Multiracial Identity in California." *Journal of Black Studies* 42, no. 3 (2011): 402–426.

Rosenblatt, Paul, Terri A. Karis, and Richard Powell. *Multiracial Couples: Black and White Voices: Understanding Families.* Thousand Oaks, CA: Sage Publications, 1995.

Spencer, Rainier. "Assessing Multiracial Identity Theory and Politics: The Challenge of Hypodescent." *Ethnicities* 4, no. 3 (2004): 357–379.

Suyemoto, K. "Racial/Ethnic Identities and Related Attributed Experiences of Multiracial Japanese European Americans." *Journal of Multicultural Counseling and Development* 32, no. 4 (2004): 206–221.

Varzally, Allison. "Review: The Shifting Grounds of Race: Black and Japanese Americans in the Making of a Multiethnic Los Angeles." *Pacific Historical Review* 78, no. 2 (2009): 305.

Wardle, Francis. "Meeting the Needs of Multiracial and Multiethnic Children in Early Childhood Settings." *Early Childhood Education Journal* 26, no. 1 (1998): 7–11.

Wehrly, Bea, Kelley Kenney, and Mark Kenney. *Counseling Multiracial Families.* Thousand Oaks, CA: Sage Publications, 1999.

References

CHAPTER 1

Census Scope. "Multiracial Population Statistics." 2009. http://www
.censusscope.org/us/chart_multi.html.

Census: Whites Make Up Minority of Babies in U.S. *USA Today*, June 23,
2011:1.

DaCosta, Kimberly McClain. *Making Multiracials: State, Family, and
Market in the Redrawing of the Color Line*. Stanford, CA: Stanford
University Press, 2007.

Daniel, G. Reginald. "Multiracial Identity in Global Perspective: The
United States, Brazil, and South Africa." In *New Faces in a Chang-
ing America: Multiracial Identity in the 21st Century*, edited by
Loretta Winters and Herman DeBose, 247–286. Thousand Oaks,
CA: Sage Publications, 2003.

Root, Maria. *The Multiracial Experience: Racial Borders as the New
Frontier*. Thousand Oaks, CA: Sage Publications, 1996.

Schmitt, Eric. "Analysis of Census Finds Segregation Along with Diversity."
New York Times, April 4, 2001: A15.

U.S. Department of Commerce, United States Census 2010. *Overview of
Race and Hispanic Origin: 2010: 2010 Census Briefs*. Washington,
DC: Economics and Statistics Administration, March 2011.

Winters, Loretta, and Herman Debose. *New Faces in a Changing
America: Multiracial Identity in the 21st Century*. Thousand Oaks,
CA: Sage Publications, 2003.

CHAPTER 2

Angel, Ronald. Quoted in "Census Data Suggests Increased Acceptance of Being Multiracial." *The Daily Texan*, April 1, 2011: 1.

Census Scope. 2009. "Multiracial Population Statistics." http://www .censusscope.org/us/chart_multi.html.

"Diversity in America: Multiracials." *American Demographics*, November 2002: S19–S20.

Hirschman, Charles, Richard Alba, and Reynolds Farley. "The Meaning and Measurement of Race in the U.S. Census: Glimpses into the Future." *Demography* 37, no. 3 (2000): 381–393.

Saulny, Susan. "Census Data Presents Rise in Multiracial Population of Youths." *The New York Times*, March 24, 2011: A3.

University of Virginia Cooper Center, Demographics & Workforce Group. *U.Va Assess 2010 Census Data on Virginia's Multi-Racial Population*. March 9, 2011.

U.S. Department of Commerce, United States Census 2010. *Overview of Race and Hispanic Origin: 2010: 2010 Census Briefs*. Washington, DC: Economics and Statistics Administration, March 2011.

U.S. Department of Commerce, United States Census 2000. *The Two or More Races Population: 2000*. Washington, DC: Economics and Statistics Administration, November 2001.

CHAPTER 3

Bowles, Dorcas. "Bi-racial Identity: Children Born to African-American and White Couples." *Clinical Social Work Journal* 21, no. 4 (1993): 417–428.

Harris, David, and Jeremiah Joseph Sim. "Who Is Multiracial?" *American Sociological Review* 67, no. 4 (2002): 614–627.

Kerwin, Christine, Joseph Ponterotto, Barbara Jackson, and Abigail Harris. "Racial Identity in Biracial Children: A Qualitative Investigation." *Journal of Counseling Psychology* 40, no. 2 (1993): 221–231.

Lee, Jennifer, and Frank Bean. "Reinventing the Color Line: Immigration and America's New Racial/Ethnic Divide." *Social Forces* 86, no. 2 (2007): 561–586.

Poll. *USA Today*, March 9, 2001: 2.

Root, Maria. "Five Mixed-Race Identities." In *New Faces in a Changing America: Multiracial Identity in the 21st Century*, edited by Loretta Winters and Herman DeBose, 3–20. Thousand Oaks, CA: Sage Publications, 2003.

Root, Maria. *The Multiracial Experience: Racial Borders as the New Frontier*. Thousand Oaks, CA: Sage Publications, 1995: 5.

Tafoya, Sonya, Hans Johnson, and Laura Hill. "Who Chooses to Choose Two?" In *The American People: Census 2000*, edited by Reynolds Farley and John Haaga, 332–351. Thousand Oaks, CA: Russell Sage Foundation, 2005.

Winters, Loretta, and Herman DeBose. *New Faces in a Changing America: Multiracial Identity in the 21st Century*. Thousand Oaks, CA: Sage Publications, 2003.

Xie, Yu, and Kimberly Goyette. "The Racial Identification of Biracial Children with One Asian Parent." *Social Forces* 76, no. 2 (1997): 547–570.

CHAPTER 4

Alderman, Bruce. *Interracial Relationships*. Detroit: Greenhaven Press, 2007.

Baird-Olson, Karen. "Colonization, Cultural Imperialism, and the Social Construction of American Indian Mixed-Blood Identity." In *New Faces in a Changing America: Multiracial Identity in the 21st Century*, edited by Loretta Winters and Herman DeBose, 194–221 Thousand Oaks, CA: Sage Publications, 2003.

Harris, Marvin. *Patterns of Race in the Americas*. Westport, CT: Greenwood, 1964.

Ifekwunigwe, Jayne. *Mixed Race Studies*. New York: Routledge, 2004.

Molnar, Stephen. *Races, Types and Ethnic Groups: The Problem of Human Variation*. Englewood Cliffs, NJ: Prentice Hall, 1975.

Morning, Ann. "New Faces, Old Faces: Counting the Multiracial Population Past and Present." In *New Faces in a Changing America: Multiracial Identity in the 21st Century*, edited by Loretta Winters and Herman DeBose, 41–67. Thousand Oaks, CA: Sage Publications, 2003.

Murphy, Christopher. *Black and White: The Relevance of Race: Unfinished Business*. Research paper, Augusta State University, Department of History and Anthropology, October 5, 2001.

Nimmons, Svenya. *Just Because I'm Mixed Doesn't Mean I'm Confused: Empowering Within and Discovering Your Heritage*. Lexington, KY: Swirlpower, 2011.

Sanabria, Harry. *The Anthropology of Latin America and the Caribbean*. Boston, MA: Pearson, 2007.

Sweet, Frank. *Legal History of the Color Line: The Rise and Triumph of the One-Drop Rule*. Palm Coast, FL: Backintyme Publications, 2005.

U.S. Census Bureau. *Population and Housing Inquiries in U.S. Decennial Census, 1790–1970*. Washington, DC: U.S. Government Printing Office, 1973.

Velazco Y Trianosky, Gregory. "Beyond Mestizaje: The Future of Race in America." In *New Faces in a Changing America: Multiracial Identity in the 21st Century*, edited by Loretta Winters and Herman DeBose, 176–193. Thousand Oaks, CA: Sage Publications, 2003.

Williamson, Joel. *New People: Miscegenation and Mulattoes in the United States*. Baton Rouge, LA: Louisiana State University Press, 1980.

Winters, Loretta, and Herman DeBose. *New Faces in a Changing America: Multiracial Identity in the 21st Century*. Thousand Oaks, CA: Sage Publications, 2003.

Zack, Naomi. *Race and Mixed Race*. Philadelphia: Temple University Press, 1993.

CHAPTER 5

Davis, F. James. *Who Is Black?* University Park, PA: Pennsylvania University Press, 1991.

Gates, Henry Louis. *Figures in Black: Words, Signs, and the "Racial" Self*. Oxford: Oxford University Press, 1989.

Gates, Henry Louis. *The Signifying Monkey: A Theory of Afro-American Literary Criticism*. Oxford: Oxford University Press, 1989.

Harris, Marvin. *Patterns of Race in the Americas*. Connecticut: Greenwood Publishing Group, 1964.

Kottack, Conrad. *Cultural Anthropology: Appreciating Cultural Diversity*. New York: McGraw-Hill, 2011.

Sweet, Frank. *Legal History of the Color Line: The Rise and Triumph of the One-Drop Rule*. Palm Coast, FL: Backintyme, 2005.

Williamson, Joel. *New People: Miscegenation and Mulattoes in the United States*. Baton Rouge, LA: Louisiana State University Press, 1980.

Zack, Naomi. *American Mixed Race: The Culture of Microdiversity*. Lanham, MD: Rowman & Littlefield, 1995.

Zack, Naomi. *Race and Mixed Race*. Philadelphia: Temple University Press, 1993.

CHAPTER 6

Altabe, Madeline. "Ethnicity and Body Image: Quantitative and Qualitative Analysis." *International Journal of Eating Disorders* 23 (1998): 153–159.

Bailey, Eric. *Black America, Body Beautiful: How the African American Image Is Changing Fashion, Fitness, and Other Industries*. Westport, CT: Praeger, 2008.

Blended People of America. "Mixed Race People Most Attractive and Successful as Say the British." July 28, 2010.

D'Souza, Nandini. "Mistaken for the Nanny: Indian-American Writer Nandini D'Souza Comes to Terms with the Playground Politics of Raising a Mixed-Race Daughter." *Bazar*, July 23, 2010: 123.

Lewis, Michael. "Why Are Mixed-Race People Perceived as More Attractive?" *Perception* 39, no. 1 (2010): 136–138.

Miller, K., D. Gleaves, T. Hirsch, B. Green, A. Snow, and C. Corbett. "Comparisons of Body Image Dimensions by Race/Ethnicity and Gender in a University Population." *International Journal of Eating Disorders* 27 (2000): 310–316.

Office of Management and Budget. *Revisions to the Standards for the Classification of Federal Data on Race and Ethnicity*. Washington, DC: The White House, 1977.

Scupin, Raymond. *Race and Ethnicity: An Anthropological Focus on the United States and the World*. Upper Saddle River, NJ: Prentice Hall, 2003.

Yang, C., P. Gray, and H. Pope. "Male Body Image in Taiwan versus the West: Yanggang Ahiqui Meets the Adonis Complex." *American Journal of Psychiatry* 162, no. 2 (2002): 263–269.

CHAPTER 7

Bailey, Eric. *Food Choice and Obesity in Black America: Creating a New Cultural Diet*. Westport, CT: Praeger, 2006.

Bailey, Eric. *Medical Anthropology and African American Health*. Westport, CT: Bergin & Garvey, 2000.

Centers for Disease Control and Prevention (CDC). "Achievements in Public Health, 1900–1999: Healthier Mothers and Babies." *Morbidity and Mortality Weekly Report* 48 (1999): 849–858.

Centers for Disease Control & Prevention (CDC). "CDC Health Disparities and Inequalities Report—United States, 2011." *Morbidity and Mortality Weekly Report* Supplement 60, January 14, 2011.

Centers for Disease Control and Prevention (CDC). "Current Trends Update on Acquired Immune Deficiency Syndrome (AIDS)— United States." *Morbidity and Mortality Weekly Report* 31 (1982): 507–508; 513–514.

Centers for Disease Control and Prevention (CDC). *Facts about HIV/ AIDS and Race/Ethnicity*. Washington, DC: U.S. Government Printing Office, 1993.

Centers for Disease Control and Prevention (CDC). "HIV Prevalence Estimates—United States, 2006." *Morbidity and Mortality Weekly Report* 57 (2008): 1073–1076.

Centers for Disease Control and Prevention (CDC). "Prevalence of Overweight and Obesity Among Adults: United States, 1999." Available at: http://www.cdc.gov/nchs/products/pubs/pubd/hestats/obese/ obse99.htm.

Flegal, K. M., M. D. Carroll, R. J. Kuczmarski, and C. I. Johnson. "Overweight and Obesity in the United States: Prevalence and Trends, 1960–1994." *International Journal of Obesity Related Metabolism Disorders* 22 (1998): 39–47.

Freedman, David. "Obesity—United States, 1988–2008." *Morbidity and Mortality Weekly Report* 60 (2011): 73–76.

Guyer, B., M. A. Freedman, D. M. Strobino, and E. J. Sondik. "Annual Summary of Vital Statistics: Trends in the Health of Americans during the 20th Century." *Pediatrics* 106 (2000): 1307–1317.

Hall, H. Irene, Denise Hughes, Hazel Dean, Jonathan Mermin, and Kevin Fenton. "HIV Infection—United States, 2005 and 2008." *Morbidity and Mortality Weekly Report* 60 (2011): 87–89.

Hall, H. I., R. Song, P. Rhodes, et al. "Estimation of HIV Incidence in the United States." *Journal of the American Medical Association* 300 (2008): 520–529.

MacDorman, Marian, and T. J. Mathews. "Infant Deaths." *Morbidity and Mortality Weekly Report* 60 (2011): 49–50.

McNeil, Donald. "Broad Racial Disparities Seen in Americans' Ills." *The New York Times*, January 14, 2011: A14.

Mokdad, A., Serdula, M., Dietz, W., Bowman, B., Marks, J., and Koplan, J. "The Spread of the Obesity Epidemic in the United States, 1991–1998." *Journal of the American Medical Association* 282 (1999): 1519–1522.

Office of Minority Health and Health Disparities (OMHD), Centers for Disease Control and Prevention (CDC). "Multiracial Populations." 2012. http://www.cdc.gov/omhd/populations/Multiracial.htm.

Phillips, Elizabeth, Adebola Odunlami, and Venice Bonham. "Mixed Race: Understanding Difference in the Genome Era." *Social Forces* 86, no. 2 (2007): 795–820.

U.S. Department of Health and Human Services. "HHS Announces Plan to Reduce Health Disparities." http://minorityhealth.hhs.gov/npa/templates/content.aspx?lvl=1&lvlid=39&ID=2892011.

CHAPTER 8

Bergstrom, Ted, Rod Garratt, and Damien Sheehan-Connor. *Stem Cell Donor Matching for Patients of Mixed Race*. Presentation at ASSA Winter Meetings, January 8, 2011.

Boodman, Sandra. "Multiracial Patients Struggle to Find Donors for Bone Marrow Transplants." *The Washington Post*, June 1, 2010: E1.

British National Party Newsroom. "Bone Marrow Donor Disparities Reveal Reality of Race Once Again." June 24, 2010: 1

CBS News. "Marrow Donors Rare for Mixed Race Patients." May 27, 2009, http://www.cbsnews.com/stories/2009/05/27/health/main5044251.shtml.

Fredrickson, Mark. "The Race to Save Nick Glasgow." 2009. http://mark frederison.wordpress.com.

Hernandez, Christina. "As Population Diversifies, Millions Are without Bone Marrow Donors." *SmartPlanet*, July 20, 2010: 1.

MatchDevan. "Be Devan's Match. Save His Life." http://www.match devan.com, 2001.

MedlinePlus, "Bone Marrow Transplant" United States National Library of Medicine, *National Library of Medicine*, 2011.

Mixed Marrow Organization. 2011. http://www.mixedmarrow.org.

National Marrow Donor Program's Be the Match Registry. Reports and Statistics. 2011. http://insidemdp/UPDATES/Reports/Documents/2010_Facts_and_Figures_Final1.pdf

Stevens, Jean. "Group Holds Marrow-Thon to Find Multiracial Donors." *The Daily Orange News*, November 13, 2002: 1–2.

Transplant News. "Mixed Race Patients Struggle to Find Bone Marrow Donor" 19, no. 7 (2009): 1.

CHAPTER 9

Baden, Amanda, and Robbie Steward. "A Framework for Use with Racially and Culturally Integrated Families: The Cultural-Racial

Identity Model as Applied to Transracial Adoption." *Journal of Social Distress and the Homeless* 9, no. 4 (2000): 309–337.

Berger, Carolyn. "Transracial Adoption: It Will Change Your Family Forever." *Multiracial Family Blog*, March 22, 2011.

Clemetson, Lynette, and Ron Nixon. "Overcoming Adoption's Racial Barriers." *The New York Times*, August 17, 2006.

McRoy, Ruth, and Christine Hall. "Transracial Adoption." In *The Multiracial Experience: Racial Borders as the New Frontier*, edited by Maria P. Root, 63–78. Thousand Oaks, CA: Sage Publications, 1996.

McRoy, Ruth, and L. Zurcher. *Transracial and Inracial Adoptees: The Adolescent Years*. Springfield, IL: Charles C. Thomas, 1983.

Morgenstern, J. "The New Face of Adoption." *Newsweek*, September 13, 1971, 67–72.

Multiracial Sky.com. "Families Created Through Transracial Adoption." 2011.

Open Arms Adoption Network. "Transracial Adoption: Becoming a Multi-Racial Family." 2011.

Ruby, Ille. "Transracial Adoption Leads to Stares: How One Mother Deals." *Parentdish*, November 4, 2010.

Samuels, Gina. "Being Raised by White People: Navigating Racial Difference among Adopted Multiracial Adults." *Journal of Marriage and Family* 71 (2009): 80–94.

Simon, R. "Adoption of Black Children by White Parents in the USA." In *Adoption Essays in Social Policy, Law, and Sociology*, edited by P. Bean, 229–242. London/New York: Tavistock, 1984.

Steward, R. J., and Amanda Baden. *The Cultural-Racial Identity Model: Understanding the Racial Identity and Cultural Identity Development of Transracial Adoptees* (Report No. UD030909). East Lansing, MI: Michigan State University. ERIC Document Reproduction Service No. ED 39 50 76, 1995.

CHAPTER 10

ABC News. "Political Punch: Before 25,000 in Dublin, Obama 'of the Moneygall Obamas' Celebrates His Irish Ancestry." http://blogs.abcnews.co/politicalpunch. Accessed May 23, 2011.

Beltran, Mary. "The New Hollywood Racelessness: Only the Fast, Furious, (and Multiracial) Will Survive." *Cinema Journal* 44, no. 2 (2005): 55–67.

Christine, James. "Cameron Diaz: Bringing a Woman's Tough to *Any Given Sunday*." Reel.com. Archived from the original on December 10, 2007. Accessed June 5, 2011.

Derek Jeter.com. http://derekjeter.mlb.co/players/jeter_derek/turn2/overview.jsp. Accessed June 13, 2011.

Freydkin, Donna. "Natalie Portman Is Force for Change, Empowering Women." *USA Today*, June 8, 2008: 1.

Hines Ward.com. http://www.hinesward.com/helping-hands-foundation.php. Accessed June 13, 2011.

Jaskolaski, Eric. "A Letter to Our 'Mixed' President" NoMoreRace.wordpress.com. http://nomorerace.wordpress.com/2010/01/02/a-letter-to-our-mixed-president/. Accessed February 3, 2011.

Look to the Stars.org. "Alicia Keys." http://www.looktothestars.org/celebrity/409-alicia-keys. Accessed June 12, 2011.

Look to the Stars.org. "Cameron Diaz." http://www.looktothestars.org/celebrity/32-cameron-diaz. Accessed June 11, 2011.

Look to the Stars.org. "Dwayne Johnson." http://www.looktothestars.org/celebrity/549-dwayne-johnson. Accessed June 9, 2011.

Look to the Stars.org. "Mariah Carey." http://www.looktothestars.org/celebrity/598-mariah-carey. Accessed June 12, 2011.

Look to the Stars.org. "Natalie Portman." http://www.looktothestars.org/celebrity/225-natalie-portman. Accessed June 8, 2011.

Look to the Stars.org. "Rosario Dawson." http://www.looktothestars.org/celebrity/500-rosario-dawson. Accessed June 12, 2011.

Milo Gladstein Foundation.org. "Bloom's Syndrome Foundation." http://www.milogladsteinfoundation.org. Accessed June 8, 2011.

Multiracial Heritage Week. http://www.facebook.com/pages/Multiracial-Heritage-Week-June-12-June18-2011/121791. Accessed February 5, 2011.

National Medical Association. "Bloom Syndrome." http://ghr.nlm.nih.gov/condition/bloom-syndrome. Accessed January 22, 2013:1.

One Race Global Foundation. http://www.causes.com/causes/351503. Accessed June 5, 2011.

Pangea Day.org. http://www.pangeaday.org. Accessed June 1, 2011.

Pittswiley. "Obama Checks 'African American' on Census, Sets Back Postracial Movement 400 Years/" *The ROOT*. http://www.theroot.co/print/40401. Accessed June 14, 2011.

Robinson, Eugene. "The Moment for This Messenger?" *Washington Post*, March 13, 2007. http://www.washingtonpost.com/wp-kyn/content/article/2007/03/12/AR2007031200983.html.

VinDiesel.com. http://www.vindiesel.com. Accessed June 5, 2011.

Votolatino.org. http://www.votolatino.org. Accessed June 12, 2011.

Wallace-Wells, Benjamin. "The Great Black Hope: What's Riding on Barack Obama?" *Washington Monthly*, November 2004. http://www.washingtonmonthly.com/features/2004/0411.wallace-wells.html.

http://www.vindiesel.com

http://www.natalieportman.com

http://www.facebook.com/DwayneJohnson

http://www.cameron-diaz.com

http://rosario-dawson.net

http://aliciakeys.com

http://mariahcarey.com

http://derekjeter.mlb.com/players/jeter_derek/index.jsp

http://web.tigerwoods.com/index

http://articles.cnn.com/2010-05-13/living/soledad.obrien.heritage_1_latinos-stories-newspaper-reporters?_s=PM:LIVING

http://ethnicelebs.com/ann-curry

http://www.hinesward.com

CHAPTER 11

Baird-Olson, Karen. "Colonization, Cultural Imperialism, and the Social Construction of American Indian Mixed Blood Identity." In *New Faces in a Changing America: Multiracial Identity in the 21st Century*, edited by Loretta Winters and Herman DeBose, 194–221. Thousand Oaks, CA: Sage Publications, 2003.

Barnes, Taylor. "For the First Time, Blacks Outnumber Whites in Brazil." *The Miami Herald*, May 24, 2011: 1.

Daniel, G. "Multiracial Identity in Global Perspective: The United States, Brazil, and South Africa." In *New Faces in a Changing America: Multiracial Identity in the 21st Century*, edited by Loretta Winters and Herman DeBose, 247–286. Thousand Oaks, CA: Sage Publications, 2003.

Hafu Japanese.org. http://www.hafujapanese.org. Accessed July 28, 2010.

Ikeda, Stewart. "The New Traditional Family." In *Interracial Relationships*, edited by Bruce Alderman, 87–94. Detroit, MI: Greenhaven Press, 2007.

King, Rebecca, and Kimberly DaCosta. "Changing Face, Changing Race: The Remaking of Race in the Japanese American and African American Communities." In *The Multiracial Experience: Racial*

Borders as the New Frontier, edited by Maria P. Root, 227–244. Thousand Oaks, CA: Sage Publications, 1996.

Mixed in Different Shades.net, http://mixedindifferentshades.net. Accessed July 21, 2010.

Nimmons, Svenya. *Just Because I'm Mixed Doesn't Mean I'm Confused: Empowering Within and Discovering Your Heritage.* Lexington, KY: Swirlpower, 2011.

Rogers, Simon. "Non-white British Population Reaches 9.1 Million." *The Guardian*, May 19, 2011: 1.

Sanabria, Harry. *The Anthropology of Latin America and the Caribbean.* Boston, MA: Pearson, 2007.

CHAPTER 13

Serling, Rod. *Twilight Zone* [Television series]. 1959.

Index